PORTRAIT OF A PROPHET'S WIFE

Emma Hale Smith

PORTRAIT OF A PROPHET'S WIFE

Emma Hale Smith

NORMA J. FISCHER

SILVER
LEAF
PRESS

Portrait of a Prophet's Wife: Emma Hale Smith

Silver Leaf Press is a division of Aspen Books.
No portion of this book may be reproduced in any form without written
permission from the publisher, Silver Leaf Press, 6211 South 380 West,
Salt Lake City, UT 84107

Library of Congress Cataloging-in-Publication Data

    Fischer, Norma J. (Norma Jones), 1918-
        Portrait of a prophet's wife : Emma Hale Smith / Norma J. Fischer.
        p.   cm.
        Includes bibliographical references and index.
        ISBN 1-56236-207-0 : $12.95
        1. Smith, Emma Hale. 2. Mormons—United States—Biography.
    3. Smith, Joseph, 1805-1844—Marriage. I. Title.
    BX8695.S515F57 1992
    289.3'092—dc20
    [B]   92-35990
                                                                  CIP

Printed in the United States of America

10   9   8   7   6   5   4   3   2   1

Cover painting: Dale Kilborne

Cover design: Richard Holdaway

LOVINGLY DEDICATED

To My Grandchildren:
Jonathan, David, Matthew, Aaron,
Angela, Melinda, Adam, Jennifer,
Daniel, Sarah, Michelle, Cherie
Anne, Joseph, and Stephen.

Emma Hale Smith

The Prophet Joseph Smith

Contents

Illustrations

1. *Restoration of the Relief Society*, by Dale Kilborne. Copyright The Church of Jesus Christ of Latter-day Saints. Used by permission. (Cover illustration.)

2. Emma Hale Smith. Courtesy Aspen Books. Used by permission. (Page vi)

3. The Prophet Joseph Smith. Courtesy Aspen Books. Used by permission. (Page vii)

4. *Emma Smith, The Elect Lady of the Restoration*, by Theodore Gorka. Copyright The Church of Jesus Christ of Latter-day Saints. Used by permission. (Page 56)

5. *Emma's Deathbed Vision*, by Dee Jay Bawden. Copyright Lyndon Cook. Used by permission. (Page 120)

6. Burial site of Joseph, Emma, and Hyrum Smith. Photographer Sheridan R. Sheffield. Used by permission. (Page 131)

Preface

While I was writing the book *Portrait of a Prophet* (a biography of the Prophet Joseph Smith published by Bookcraft, 1960), I gained a great deal of love and sympathy for Joseph's wife, Emma Hale Smith. I was inspired by the many occasions throughout his life when the Prophet Joseph Smith expressed his love and concern for his "Affectionate Emma."

In choosing materials to paint a portrait of Emma in this book, I have gone to her friends. If you want to know a person's true character, you should go to the friends, not the enemies. Emma's friends knew her best, because they knew the true thoughts of her heart.

The Thirteenth Article of Faith of The Church of Jesus Christ of Latter-day Saints says, ". . . If there is anything virtuous, lovely or of good report or praiseworthy, we seek after these things." In writing this book, I have sought those things in Emma's life that were virtuous, lovely and of good report and praiseworthy. Many of Emma's virtues can be verified. As you read this book, I hope that you also will admire these virtues.

Acknowledgements

Over a period of many years, numerous people have helped me in my quest to obtain positive historical material about the Prophet Joseph Smith's wife, Emma. It would be difficult, if not impossible, to mention the names of all those who have been very kind in giving me help and advice, but I would like to give special thanks to three Brigham Young University professors who have given me the most recent help in the preparation of the final manuscript for this book. They are Don E. Norton, Larry C. Porter, and V. Ben Bloxham.

I wish to extend my sincere thanks and appreciation to the publishing companies and authors listed in the reference notes for their kind permission to use quoted material. I would also like to express my appreciation to my husband, Wilford A. Fischer, for his constant encouragement and his help in proofreading quoted material.

PORTRAIT OF A PROPHET'S WIFE

Emma Hale Smith

I

The Visions

"More things are wrought by prayer than this world dreams of."

—*Alfred Lord Tennyson*[1]

*I*n October 1825, the Prophet Joseph Smith met the most faithful friend he would ever have in his short life—Emma Hale, a beautiful girl, twenty-one years of age. She was "a brunette with luminous eyes, intelligent, and capable."[2] "There was nothing of arrogance about her, but there was a gentle dignity."[3] She knew and practiced the social graces she learned at an academy for girls she had attended; and she had also taught school in Harmony, Pennsylvania. In addition to her academic and social achievements, she was gifted in music. She had a beautiful lyric soprano voice and "sang in the village choir."[4]

Emma was the daughter of Isaac Hale, a well-to-do farmer who lived in Harmony, Pennsylvania. She was born on July 10, 1804, the seventh in a family of nine children. Isaac Hale was a prosperous farmer and a stalwart citizen of Harmony. At the time Emma met Joseph, Isaac Hale was a member of the Methodist Church. He had not always been a devout Methodist, but he had always believed in God. He became active in the Methodist faith after he stopped by the woods one day and saw little Emma, who was then about seven or eight years old, praying that her father would have a faith in Christ like she had. Isaac Hale was touched by the simple faith of his young daughter.[5]

In addition to being a farmer, Isaac Hale and his wife and family owned and managed a boarding house. It was here that Emma met Joseph Smith, who had come to Harmony to help Josiah Stoal in a mining project.[6] Joseph was accepted as a boarder in Isaac Hale's boarding house. Joseph was a handsome young man, tall, fair-complexioned, with piercing blue eyes and a religious nature.

Joseph admired Emma from the time he first saw her. Her religious nature was like his own. He knew he could trust her with his innermost feelings. He told Emma about what had happened to him when he was just a fourteen-year-old boy trying to decide which church he should join.

Joseph described to her how he had gone alone into a grove of trees to pray, wanting to know which church was true. In answer to his prayer, God the Father and his Son, Jesus Christ, appeared to him, revealing to Joseph that all of the churches had gone astray of the true gospel and that he should join none of them. He was told to continue as he had until further knowledge was given him. (See Pearl of Great Price, Joseph Smith–History.)

Joseph told Emma that from the age of fourteen to the age of seventeen, he continued to pursue his "common vocations" in life. His most "common vocation" was helping his parents and brothers and sisters on the farm. At this time they were also struggling to build a house for themselves. Then, on the night of September 21, 1823, when he was earnestly praying, he saw the second of his marvelous visions.

An angel, who called himself Moroni, appeared to Joseph at his bedside and said that God had a work for him to do. He showed Joseph the location of an ancient record that had been compiled by prophets from this continent. He also described the Urim and Thummin, a tool given to the ancient prophets by God to help them translate works from other languages. Joseph was told that he would find these objects in a stone box buried on a nearby hill—the Hill Cumorah. The angel appeared to Joseph three times that night, each time giving more instruction. The next morning as Joseph went out to work, his strength failed him and he fell unconscious near a fence in the field. The angel appeared to him again, directing him to go to his father and relate the experiences of the previous night. Joseph did and was told by his father that all this was of the Lord and that he should do as the angel directed. Joseph then made his way to the hill where the record was deposited.

Joseph was not allowed to take the record, but he was able to open the stone box in which it lay and look at it. He said that the record had the appearance of gold and was made up of metal plates bound by three large rings. On them was inscribed characters of a foreign language. Joseph was told to return to the hill next year on that same date.

Joseph told Emma that on each September 22 for three years, he had gone to the place where the Golden Plates were deposited, and each time he had received "instruction and intelligence" from the heavenly messenger.

Emma believed all that Joseph told her. Joseph knew then that Emma could be his true and trusted friend.

During the next fifteen months, from October 1825 to January 1827, the friendship between Emma and Joseph ripened into love. Joseph was now twenty-one years of age, and he wanted to marry Emma who was twenty-two. They were both old enough to get married without their parents' consent.

However, in deference to his parents, Joseph told them about his desire to marry Emma. His parents knew Emma and loved her, so Joseph knew that he would have no difficulty in getting his parents' approval of his marriage. When he told his parents his intentions, they not only approved but asked Joseph to bring Emma to Manchester to live with the Smith family after their marriage.

To propose marriage to Emma was not difficult, because Joseph knew how much she loved him. The most difficult thing Joseph had to do was to ask Isaac Hale for his daughter's hand in marriage. As Joseph had anticipated, Emma's father was very much opposed to the marriage. He did not want his daughter to marry Joseph, because Joseph would not deny his visions, nor would he deny his subsequent visits with the angel Moroni at the Hill Cumorah. Isaac Hale knew that if his daughter married Joseph, she too would be ridiculed and persecuted as Joseph had been after people had heard about his visions and his visits from the angel Moroni.

Emma loved Joseph, and she was courageous enough to face persecution for the sake of righteousness, as Joseph had been. Therefore, she went with Joseph to the house of Esquire Zachariah Tarbell, justice of the peace, in South Bainbridge, New York, and there they were married, on January 18, 1827. Then, as Joseph's parents had requested, they went to Manchester, New York, to live with the Smith family.

II

The Golden Plates

"The Book of Mormon is the most correct of any book on earth, and the keystone of our religion. A man would get nearer to God by abiding by its precepts, than by any other book."

—*Joseph Smith*

Joseph Smith was instructed by angel Moroni to meet him at the Hill Cumorah on September 22 of each year to see the golden plates and obtain further instructions.[1] Joseph had met Moroni at the Hill Cumorah each year for three consecutive years. Joseph did so until September 22, 1827. This fourth visit was different from the previous appearances, because Joseph was now married; therefore, he was able to take his wife with him. They left the Smith home just after midnight in a wagon that belonged to Joseph Knight, Sr., who was visiting with the Smith family in Manchester.

As they came close to the Hill Cumorah, Joseph told Emma that he thought it would be better for him to go the rest of the way alone. Emma accepted Joseph's decision and said she would wait for him in the wagon.

When Joseph returned to the wagon where Emma was waiting for him, he was carrying the golden plates wrapped in his coat. As they drove home Joseph must have considered the great responsibility that was now his in protecting and translating the precious plates. He thought of Moroni's words of admonition when he accepted this great responsibility:

> Now you have got the Record into your own hands, and you are but a man, therefore you will have to be watchful and faithful to your trust, or you will be overpowered by wicked men; for they will lay every plan and scheme that is possible to get it away from you, and if you do not take heed continually they will succeed. While it was in my hands, I could keep it, and no man had power to take it away! But now I give it up to you. Beware, and look well to your ways, and you shall have power to retain it, until the time for it to be translated.[2]

News that Joseph had obtained the golden plates from Moroni traveled rapidly. "Wicked men" disrupted the Smith family's household many times trying to get the golden plates away from him.[3] Emma was as eager as Joseph to protect the plates and keep them safe and out of the hands of such men.

It was difficult for Joseph to translate the plates in Manchester, New York, because of this interference. Where could Joseph find the peace and safety he needed in order to do the important work of translating? He would find it in Harmony, Pennsylvania.

Isaac Hale invited Joseph and Emma to come to Harmony and live with the Hale family. Considering Isaac Hale's hostility toward Joseph when Joseph eloped with Emma, why did Isaac Hale invite the couple to come live with the Hale family? Cecil McGavin, in his book *The Family of Joseph Smith*, gives an answer to this question. He says that Isaac Hale invited his estranged daughter back to her home in Harmony so that the whole Hale family could work on her and "convince her of her terrible folly" in marrying Joseph, and in this way perhaps separate Joseph and Emma and bring Emma back to her family and "into the Methodist fold."[4]

After arriving in Harmony, Joseph and Emma lived for a short time with the Hale family. During this time the Hale family was not successful in "convincing Emma of her folly" in marrying Joseph.

In Joseph Smith's time a boarding house such as the Hale family owned was also called an inn or a tavern. It was a busy place, frequented by many people. Consequently it did not give Emma and Joseph the privacy they needed to begin the translation of the golden plates. Thus Joseph made arrangements with Isaac Hale to purchase thirteen acres of land with a small frame house on it. Isaac Hale had called this house his pelt house because he had used it to store "the hides of deer and other wild game until they were sold or tanned and made into useful articles."[5] After Joseph had completed the business of purchasing the small house and the land from Isaac Hale, he and Emma renovated the little house for use as their home in Harmony.

In the move from Manchester to Harmony, Joseph and Emma put the sacred plates in a barrel filled with beans to protect them from enemies. The plates may have been kept in this barrel until the small house became the home of Joseph and Emma.

The Spirit of the Lord blessed this humble home of Joseph and Emma, and it became a sacred sanctuary for the golden plates. With the use of the Urim and Thummim which had been deposited with the plates, Joseph began translating the history contained on the record. Emma helped him by serving as his scribe.

Moroni had instructed Joseph not to show the golden plates to anyone until he had finished the translation. Therefore, Joseph had a curtain placed between him and his scribe, so that the scribe could hear his voice but not see the plates.

Why wasn't Emma allowed to see the plates? No doubt Joseph wanted to show them to her, but the time to provide witnesses to verify the authenticity of the golden plates had not arrived. This would come later, after the plates had been translated. But Emma did not have to see the plates to be convinced of their authenticity. She had great faith. She was not like "Doubting Thomas," who had to see before he could believe. Jesus said to Thomas, "Because thou hast seen me, thou hast believed. Blessed are they that have not seen, and yet have believed." (John 20:29.)

Emma not only had great faith, but she also had great fidelity. The golden plates were kept covered on a table in their humble home in Harmony. Emma moved them when she did her housework, but she never uncovered them to see them. This is verified by what Emma told her son, Joseph III, in later years:

> I moved them from place to place on the table, as it became necessary in doing my work. . . . I once felt of the plates as they lay on the table, tracing their outline and shape. They seemed to be pliable like thick paper and would rattle with a metallic sound when the edges were moved by the thumb. I did not attempt to handle the plates other than I have told you, nor uncover them to look at them. I was satisfied that it was the work of God, and therefore, did not feel it necessary to do so.[6]

When Emma was expecting her first baby, her health and household duties made it difficult for her to spend very much time as Joseph's scribe. Joseph needed someone who would be able to help him continually in this very important work of translation. Finally he was able to get Martin Harris, who lived in Palmyra, New York, and who was a very good friend of the Smith family, to come to Harmony to be his scribe. Joseph and Martin worked on the translation diligently until one hundred sixteen pages were completed. Then Martin asked for permission to take the manuscript to Palmyra to show it to his family.

Joseph inquired of the Lord to know if it would be all right for him to grant Martin's request. The Lord's answer was no. Martin, not satisfied, asked Joseph to inquire again, but still the answer was no. He insisted that Joseph inquire a third time, and this time the answer was that Martin Harris could take the manuscript with him to Palmyra if he would promise to show it to no one except five specific persons in his family whom the Lord named. Martin, delighted with this answer, bound himself with a written covenant that he would show the manuscript to no one except those people. Martin then took the manuscript to Palmyra.

After Martin left, Joseph became very uneasy, fearing that Martin would not keep his promise.

Joseph's and Emma's first child, a son, was born on June 15, 1828, while Martin was away on this trip to Palmyra. The little child died the day it was born. This was a great sorrow for Emma and Joseph. Emma was also very ill after the birth, and at times Joseph felt he might lose his wife, just as he had lost his little son, whom they had named Alvin.

When Emma's health began to improve, she became aware of Joseph's anxiety about the manuscript which Martin Harris had taken to Palmyra. She had great empathy for her husband, and she also desired that the history on the golden plates be translated as soon as possible. The fear of what Martin Harris had done with the 116-page manuscript troubled Emma also. To relieve their anxieties, Emma told Joseph that he should go to Palmyra to see what had happened to Martin and the manuscript. With Emma's assurance that she was feeling better and that she would be all right while he was gone, Joseph began the one hundred twenty-five mile trip from Harmony to Palmyra.

After Joseph arrived at his father's home in Manchester, he received the sad news that Martin Harris had broken his promise. He had shown the manuscript to more than the five people the Lord had specified, and the manuscript was lost. Joseph, overcome with grief, felt that he, too, was responsible for the loss of the manuscript because he had let Martin take it to Palmyra. Soon after Joseph returned to Harmony, he explained:

> I commenced humbling myself in mighty prayer before the Lord, and, as I was pouring out my soul in supplication to God, that if possible I might obtain mercy at his hands and be forgiven of all that I had done contrary to His will, an angel stood before me, and answered me, saying, that I had sinned in delivering the manuscript into the hands of a wicked man, and, as I had ventured to become

responsible for his faithfulness, I would of necessity have to suffer the consequences of his indiscretion, and I must now give up the Urim and Thummim into his (the angel's) hands.

This I did as I was directed, and as I handed them to him, he remarked, "If you are very humble and penitent, it may be that you will receive them again; if so, it will be on the twenty-second of next September. . . ."

After the angel left me, . . . I continued my supplication to God without cessation, and on the twenty-second of September, I had the joy and satisfaction of again receiving the Urim and Thummim, with which I have again commenced translating, and *Emma writes for me*, [emphasis added] but the angel said that the Lord would send me a scribe, and I trust His promise will be verified. The angel seemed pleased with me when he gave me back the Urim and Thummim, and he told me that the Lord loved me, for my faithfulness and humility.[7]

Again Emma became Joseph's scribe, but neither Joseph nor Emma had very much time to work on the translation, because Emma was very busy with her household duties, and most of Joseph's time was spent working on the little farm he was buying from his father-in-law, Isaac Hale, who wanted to make Joseph a responsible farmer. Emma's devotion to Joseph was clearly so great that the Hale family could not separate them.

Joseph and Emma worked on the translation in their spare time, but of course it progressed slowly. However, they did feel that the Lord was pleased with their sincere efforts to do as much as they could. The Lord advised them, "Do not run faster or labor more than you have strength and means provided to enable you to translate." (D&C 10:4.) They had faith that the Lord would provide help for them and that the translation would proceed faster in the Lord's own due time. They knew that a great and "marvelous work" was about "to come forth among the children of men." (D&C 4:1.)

Oliver Cowdery, a school teacher in Manchester, was the answer to Joseph's and Emma's prayers for help in translating the golden plates. Oliver had boarded at the home of Joseph's parents. They told him about how Joseph had come into possession of the plates. Apparently Oliver believed what the Smith family told him. He had prayed about it, but he wanted further knowledge of their authenticity. In answer to Oliver's sincere prayer, the Lord gave Oliver a testimony of the authenticity of the plates, as follows:

> Verily, verily, I say unto you, if you desire a further witness, cast your mind upon the night that you cried unto me in your heart, that you might know concerning the truth of these things.
>
> Did I not speak peace to your mind concerning the matter? What greater witness can you have than from God?
>
> And now behold, you have received a witness; for if I have told you things which no man knoweth have you not received a witness? (D&C 6:22-24.)

After Oliver received his witness from God concerning Joseph and the golden plates, he went to Harmony, Pennsylvania, and became the scribe the Lord had promised Joseph. Joseph and Oliver commenced the sacred work of translating the golden plates on April 7, 1829.

When the people in Harmony became aware of what Joseph and Oliver were doing, they became angry and tried to disrupt the work. Because of this hostility, Joseph asked Oliver to write to his friend, David Whitmer, who lived near Fayette, New York, and let him know about the difficulty they were having. Oliver asked David if he and Joseph could come to the Whitmer home, where they might have peace and safety to continue their work of translation.

David Whitmer not only agreed to let them come to Fayette to continue their work, but he also made a special trip to Harmony to bring Joseph and Oliver to the Whitmer home. His father, Peter Whitmer, Sr., seemed very interested in the work they were doing and opened his home to them.

Emma remained in Harmony until later. She was safe after Joseph and Oliver left. "Just when she moved to the Whitmer home is not definite, but it is clear that when she arrived she was received with kindly hospitality."[8]

In the latter part of June, 1829, the work of translation was completed. Joseph then sent for his father and mother to come to Peter Whitmer's home in Fayette, New York, to rejoice with him and Emma and the Whitmers and Oliver

Cowdery in this great accomplishment. Joseph also requested Martin Harris to come.

This was a glorious occasion in the lives of Oliver Cowdery, David Whitmer, and Martin Harris, because these three men were shown the golden plates by an angel of the Lord, and they were commanded to testify to the world that they had seen the golden plates from which Joseph Smith had translated the Book of Mormon.

After the three witnesses had been shown the golden plates by an angel of the Lord, Joseph felt a great burden lift from his shoulders. His great relief in having others share his burden is related by his mother, Lucy Mack Smith, as follows:

> On coming in, Joseph threw himself down beside me, and exclaimed, "Father, Mother, you do not know how happy I am: the Lord has now caused the plates to be shown to three more besides myself. They have seen an angel, who has testified to them, and they will have to bear witness to the truth of what I have said, for now they know for themselves, that I do not go about to deceive the people, and I feel as if I were relieved of a burden which was almost too heavy for me to bear, and it rejoices my soul, that I am not any longer to be entirely alone in the world."[9]

Following is the testimony of the three witnesses as recorded in the front of the Book of Mormon:

> BE IT KNOWN unto all nations, kindreds, tongues, and people, unto whom this work shall

come: That we, through the grace of God the Father, and our Lord Jesus Christ, have seen the plates which contain this record, which is a record of the people of Nephi, and also of the Lamanites, their brethren, and also of the people of Jared, who came from the tower of which hath been spoken. And we also know that they have been translated by the gift and power of God, for his voice has declared it unto us; wherefore we know of a surety that the work is true. And we also testify that we have seen the engravings which are upon the plates; and they have been shown unto us by the power of God, and not of man. And we declare with words of soberness, that an angel of God came down from heaven, and he brought and laid before our eyes, that we beheld and saw the plates, and the engravings thereon; and we know that it is by the grace of God the Father, and our Lord Jesus Christ, that we beheld and bear record that these things are true. And it is marvelous in our eyes. Nevertheless, the voice of the Lord commanded us that we should bear record of it; wherefore, to be obedient unto the commandments of God, we bear testimony of these things. And we know that if we are faithful in Christ, we shall rid our garments of the blood of all men, and be found spotless before the judgment-seat of Christ, and shall dwell with him eternally in the heavens. And the honor be to the Father, and to the Son, and to the Holy Ghost, which is one God. Amen.

OLIVER COWDERY
DAVID WHITMER
MARTIN HARRIS

After the three witnesses were shown the golden plates, the Lord permitted eight more men to see them. The testimony of these eight witnesses is recorded in the front of the Book of Mormon, as follows:

BE IT KNOWN unto all nations, kindreds, tongues, and people, unto whom this work shall come: That Joseph Smith, Jun., the translator of this work, has shown unto us the plates of which hath been spoken, which have the appearance of gold; and as many of the leaves as the said Smith had translated we did handle with our hands; and we also saw the engravings thereon, all of which has the appearance of ancient work, and of curious workmanship. And this we bear record with words of soberness, that the said Smith has shown unto us, for we have seen and hefted, and know of a surety that the said Smith has got the plates of which we have spoken. And we give our names unto the world, to witness unto the world that which we have seen. And we lie not, God bearing witness of it.

CHRISTIAN WHITMER	HIRAM PAGE
JACOB WHITMER	JOSEPH SMITH, SEN.
PETER WHITMER, JUN.	HYRUM SMITH
JOHN WHITMER	SAMUEL H. SMITH

After the witnesses had verified the authenticity of the golden plates, the Book of Mormon was published. Then The Church of Jesus Christ of Latter-day Saints was organized on April 6, 1830 at Fayette, New York.

III

The "Elect Lady"

"... Emma Smith, my daughter, ... thou art an
elect lady, whom I have called."

—*D&C 25:1, 3*

The organization of The Church of Jesus Christ of Latter-day
Saints took place on Tuesday, April 6, 1830 in the home of
Peter Whitmer, Sr., in Fayette, New York. There were six
original members: Joseph Smith, Jr., Oliver Cowdery, Hyrum
Smith, Samuel Smith, David Whitmer and Peter Whitmer, Jr.

Although many people attended this meeting, only six signed the charter, because six was enough to satisfy the legal requirements to form a society or organization in the state of New York.

The Church began to grow immediately. On June 9, 1830, the first conference of The Church of Jesus Christ of Latter-day Saints was held at the Whitmer home. Thirty members of the Church and many investigators attended.[1] In his diary, the Prophet Joseph Smith recorded the following:

> Immediately after the conference I returned to my own house, and from thence, accompanied by my wife, Oliver Cowdery, John Whitmer and David Whitmer, went again on a visit to Mr. Knight, of Colesville, Broome County. We found a number in the neighborhood still believing, and now anxious to be baptized. We appointed a meeting for the Sabbath, and on the afternoon of Saturday we erected a dam across a stream of water, which was convenient, for the purpose of there attending to the ordinance of baptism; but during the night a mob collected and tore down the dam, which hindered us from attending to the baptism on the Sabbath.[2]
>
> Early on Monday morning we were on the alert, and before our enemies were aware of our proceedings, we had repaired the dam, and the following thirteen persons baptized, by Oliver Cowdery; viz., Emma Smith, Hezekiah Peck and his wife, Joseph Knight, Sen., and wife, William Stringham and wife, Joseph Knight, Jun., Aaron Culver and wife, Levi Hale, Polly Knight, and Julia Stringham.[3]

After Emma and the others were baptized, they went to the Knight home to be confirmed, but because of mob interference and violence, no confirmation service was held at this time.

Emma was confirmed a few weeks later, in early August 1830. The Prophet Joseph Smith wrote about this important occasion as follows:

> Early in the month of August Newell Knight and his wife paid us a visit at my place in Harmony, Pennsylvania; and as neither his wife nor mine had been as yet confirmed, it was proposed that we should confirm them, and partake together of the Sacrament, before he and his wife should leave us. In order to prepare for this I set out to procure some wine for the occasion, but had gone only a short distance when I was met by a heavenly messenger, and received the following revelation:
>
> 1. Listen to the voice of Jesus Christ, your Lord, and your God, and your Redeemer, whose word is quick and powerful.
>
> 2. For, behold, I say unto you, that it mattereth not what ye shall eat, or what ye shall drink, when ye partake of the sacrament, if it so be that ye do it with an eye single to my glory—remembering unto the Father my body which was laid down for you, and my blood which was shed for the remission of your sins.
>
> 3. Wherefore, a commandment I give unto you, that you shall not purchase wine, neither strong drink of your enemies:

4. Wherefore, you shall partake of none except it is made new among you; yea, in my Father's kingdom which shall be built up on the earth. [This revelation is also recorded in Section 27, Verses 1 to 4 of the Doctrine and Covenants.][4]

In obedience to the above commandment, we prepared some wine of our own making, and held our meeting, consisting only of five, viz., Newell Knight and his wife, myself and my wife, and John Whitmer. We partook together of the Sacrament, after which we confirmed those two sisters into the Church, and spent the evening in a glorious manner. The Spirit of the Lord was poured out upon us, we praised the Lord God, and rejoiced exceedingly.[5]

In July of 1830, at Harmony, Pennsylvania, the Prophet Joseph Smith received a revelation directed to his wife, Emma. In part of this revelation, found in Section 25 of the Doctrine and Covenants, the Lord says to Emma:

A revelation I give unto you concerning my will; and if thou art faithful and walk in the paths of virtue before me, I will preserve thy life, and thou shalt receive an inheritance in Zion.

Behold, thy sins are forgiven thee, and thou art an elect lady, whom I have called.

. . . It shall be given thee . . . to make a selection of sacred hymns, . . . which is pleasing unto me, to be had in my church.

For my soul delighteth in the song of the heart; yea, the song of the righteous is a prayer unto me, and it shall be answered with a blessing upon their heads. (D&C 25:2, 3, 11, 12.)

Emma, being gifted in music, was well qualified "to make a selection of sacred hymns" for the first hymn book of The Church of Jesus Christ of Latter-day Saints.

Among the many hymns she selected are the following, which can be found in our present hymn book published in 1985:

He Died, The Great Redeemer Died
Now Let Us Rejoice
Redeemer of Israel
Guide Us, O Thou Great Jehovah
How Firm a Foundation
God is Love
Gently Raise the Sacred Strain
Come Let Us Sing an Evening Hymn
Oh God, The Eternal Father
Joy to the World
Know This, That Every Soul is Free
Now We'll Sing With One Accord
Oh God, Our Help in Ages Past
The Happy Day at Last Has Come
Come All Ye Saints of Zion
Let Zion in Her Beauty Rise
Adam-Ondi-Ahman
We're Not Ashamed to Own Our Lord
Come, All Ye Saints Who Dwell on Earth
Great is the Lord
Come, All Whose Souls Are Lighted
Glorious Things of Thee are Spoken
Jesus, Mighty King in Zion
The Spirit of God Like a Fire is Burning

After the publication of the Book of Mormon and the organization of The Church of Jesus Christ of Latter-day Saints, and the beginning of baptisms into this Church, persecutions and hostilities against the Church increased in Harmony, Pennsylvania. Nathaniel Lewis, who was Emma's uncle, was a minister of the Methodist Church in Harmony, and he was one of Joseph's worst enemies. He turned not only the neighbors against Joseph, but also Emma's father. This time Isaac Hale's hostility against Joseph was even greater than when Joseph eloped with his daughter Emma.

Because of Isaac Hale's attitude, Peter Whitmer invited Joseph and Emma to move to Fayette, New York, to live with the Whitmer family. Joseph accepted Peter's invitation, and Emma chose to go with Joseph, although this move meant that she would never see her father and mother again.

Because Emma's love and devotion for Joseph was so great, her father failed to separate them. Emma was willing to give up her family and all she had in Harmony, Pennsylvania, to follow her prophet husband through his many afflictions and persecutions. The love Emma had for Joseph might be expressed by the following nineteenth-century poem written by the famous English author, Elizabeth Barrett Browning:

> How do I love thee? Let me count the ways.
> I love thee to the depth and breadth and height
> My soul can reach, when feeling out of sight
> For the ends of Being and ideal Grace.

I love thee to the level of every day's
Most quiet need, by sun and candle-light.
I love thee freely, as men strive for Right;
I love thee purely, as they turn from Praise.
I love thee with the passion put to use
In my old griefs, and with my childhood's faith.
I love thee with a love I seemed to lose
With my lost saints,—I love thee with the breath,
Smiles, tears, of all my life!—and, if God choose,
I shall but love thee better after death.[6]

Elizabeth Barrett was a contemporary of Emma Smith, there being less than two years difference in age. Emma was born on July 10, 1804, and Elizabeth was born on March 6, 1806. Like Emma, Elizabeth Barrett had to elope when she married Robert Browning, because her father was very much opposed to her marriage. It would take a love as great as the love expressed in Elizabeth Barrett Browning's poem to endure the many hardships and vicissitudes Emma had to endure after she married the Prophet Joseph Smith.

Commenting on the depth of their love for one another, Dr. Truman G. Madsen, has said, "Joseph Smith loved her [Emma] with his whole soul. And the corollary is, Emma loved him [Joseph] with her whole soul."[7]

Professor Ivan J. Barrett, who has taught Church History at Brigham Young University for many years, relates, "Emma was devotedly attached to her husband. She endured hardship, persecution and heartache for his sake, and she did it all without a murmur. . . . Joseph's love for Emma was equally fervent. This bond of love and devotion is found throughout the Prophet's own journal."[8]

Emma said a sad farewell to her family. Then she and Joseph moved to Fayette, New York, to live with the Whitmer family. "Her farewell was a final testament to her family of her love for Joseph."[9]

After Joseph and Emma were settled in Fayette, New York, Joseph received a revelation from the Lord commanding Oliver Cowdery, Parley P. Pratt, Ziba Peterson, and Peter Whitmer, Jun., to go on a mission to Missouri and to preach the Gospel along the way. (D&C 32:1-3.) In her history of her son, Joseph Smith, Lucy Mack Smith writes:

> As soon as this revelation was received, Emma Smith, and several other sisters, began to make arrangements to furnish those who were set apart for this mission, with the necessary clothing, which was no easy task, as the most of it had to be manufactured out of the raw material.
>
> Emma's health at this time was quite delicate, yet she did not favor herself on this account, but whatever her hands found to do, she did with her might, until so far beyond her strength that she brought upon herself a heavy fit of sickness, which lasted four weeks. And, although her strength was exhausted, still her spirits were the same, which, in fact, was always the case with her, even under the most trying circumstances. I have never seen a woman in my life, who would endure every species of fatigue and hard-

ship, from month to month, and from year to year, with that unflinching courage, zeal, and patience, which she has ever done; for I know that which she has had to endure—she has been tossed upon the ocean of uncertainty—she has breasted the storms of persecution, and buffeted the rage of men and devils, which would have born down almost any other woman.[10]

Emma's health was "quite delicate" at this time because she was expecting another baby. However, the baby would not be born in Fayette, New York, where she and Joseph were at last comfortably settled. It would be born in Kirtland, Ohio, and "it" would be twins.

Missionaries had converted many people in the Kirtland area. In December 1830 the Prophet Joseph Smith received a revelation commanding that the Church "should assemble together" in Ohio. (D&C 37:3.) On January 2, 1831, Joseph Smith received another revelation saying that in Ohio the Church would be "endowed with power from on high." (D&C 38:32.)

In obedience to the Lord's commandment, Joseph and Emma left Fayette, New York, and moved to Kirtland, Ohio.

IV

Kirtland

"To me, Emma appeared to be the queen of Joseph's heart and of his home."

—*Benjamin Johnson*

On April 30, 1831, about three months after Joseph and Emma arrived in Kirtland, Ohio, Emma gave birth to twins, a boy whom they named Thaddeus, and a girl whom they named Louisa. But like their first baby, Alvin, these little twins died after only a few hours of life. Emma's sorrow was great.

God had given her three children, and death had taken them from her before she could experience the great joys of motherhood. Her sorrow softened, however, when two tiny twin babies were brought to her to take the place of her own. These twin babies were the children of John Murdock, a member of the Church whose wife had died from childbirth. Emma gladly accepted these little babies as her own; she and Joseph named them Joseph and Julia.

While these twin babies were still small, a tragic event happened to Joseph and Emma which resulted in the death of their little adopted son. This tragic event is best told in the Prophet Joseph Smith's own words which follow:

On the twenty-fifth day of March (1833) the twins, . . . which had been sick of the measles for some time, caused us to be broken of our rest in taking care of them, especially my wife. In the evening I told her she had better retire to rest with one of the children, and I would watch with the sicker child. In the night she told me I had better lie down on the trundle bed, and I did so, and was soon after awakened by her screaming murder! When I found myself going out of the door in the hands of about a dozen men; . . . I made a desperate struggle, and I was forced out. . . .

They then seized me by the throat and held on till I lost my breath. . . . They . . . fetched the bucket of tar, when one exclaimed, . . . "Let us tar up his mouth;" and they tried to force the tar paddle in my mouth; I twisted my head around so that they could not. . . . They then tried to force a vial into my mouth, and broke it in my teeth. . . .

They then left me, and I attempted to rise, but fell again; I pulled the tar away from my lips, etc., so that I could breath more freely, and after a while I began to recover and raised myself up, when I saw two lights. I made my way towards one of them and found it was Father Johnson's. When I had come to the door . . . the tar made me look as though I was covered with blood; and when my wife saw me she thought I was all mashed to pieces and fainted. . . .

My friends spent the night in scraping and removing the tar, and washing and cleansing my body, so that by morning I was ready to be clothed again. This being Sabbath morning, the people assembled for meeting at the usual hour of worship, . . . With my flesh all scarified and defaced, I preached to the congregation, as usual, and in the afternoon of the same day baptized three individuals.[1]

The little twin, Joseph, who was sick with the measles, was lying on the trundle bed with the Prophet Joseph Smith when this mob violence occurred. A few days later, this little twin died of exposure. Emma's sorrow was great, but she "had little time to remain in uninterrupted mourning. Within a week after the mobbing, Joseph left on a three-month mission to Independence, Missouri. With infant Julia in her arms, Emma took little Joseph Murdock's body in a small coffin to Kirtland where she buried her adopted son next to her own little twins."[2]

About a year after the birth and loss of her twins, Emma was expecting another baby. During most of the time she was expecting this baby, the Prophet was away on a mission to the Eastern States. An excerpt from a letter Joseph wrote to Emma at this time shows the love and deep concern he felt for her:

My dear wife, . . . the thoughts of home, of Emma, and Julia, rushes upon my mind like a flood, and I could wish for a moment to be with them. My breast is filled with all the feeling and tenderness of a parent and a husband, and could I be with you, I would tell you many things. . . . I feel as if I wanted to say something to you to comfort you in your peculiar trial and present affliction. . . . I pray God to soften the hearts of those around you to be kind to you and take the burden off your shoulders as much as possible and not afflict you. I feel for you, for I know your state and that others do not, but you must comfort yourself, knowing that God is your friend in heaven and that you have one true and living friend on Earth, your Husband.[3]

Joseph thought he would be home before the birth of his baby, but he arrived home shortly after the baby was born. The baby was born on November 6, 1832 in their apartment over the Whitney Store. They named the baby Joseph III, after his father and grandfather.

While Emma and Joseph were living in their apartment over the Whitney Store, Joseph established what was known as the "School of the Prophets." In this school the brethren studied not only the scriptures, but also languages, history and geography. During their meetings, the men smoked their pipes and chewed their tobacco. Emma did not like to clean the tobacco "mess" the brethren left after they attended the School of the Prophets. Emma told Joseph about her objection to the brethren smoking and chewing tobacco in their home. When Joseph inquired of the Lord, he received what we know now as the Word of Wisdom, a revelation found in Section 89 of the Doctrine and Covenants.

In addition to being a good housekeeper, Emma was also an excellent cook as shown by the compliment Lyman Wright, one of Joseph's and Emma's close friends, gave Emma when she and Joseph were living in Far West. He said, "Emma, with a piece of your cornbread, I could stand on the south side of the house and imagine myself in paradise."[4]

Emma was also a good mother. She kept her children neat and clean. This is illustrated by an incident that happened when Benjamin Johnson was visiting with Joseph Smith. Benjamin said that while he was having a private conversation with Joseph, two of Joseph's and Emma's children came into the room "all so nice, bright and sweet." Joseph drew Benjamin's attention to the children as he said, "Benjamin, look at these children, how could I help loving their mother." Benjamin Johnson said that to him Emma appeared to be "the queen" of Joseph's "heart and of his home."[5]

The Prophet Joseph Smith's father, Joseph Smith, Sr., was the first patriarch of the newly-organized church—The Church of Jesus Christ of Latter-day Saints. On December 9, 1834, he gave Emma the following patriarchal blessing:

> Emma, my daughter-in-law, thou art blessed of the Lord for thy faithfulness and truth. Thou shalt be blessed with thy husband, and rejoice in the glory which shall come upon him. Thy soul has been afflicted because of the wickedness of men in seeking the destruction of thy companion, and thy whole soul has been drawn out in prayer for his deliverance; rejoice, for the Lord thy God has heard thy supplication. Thou hast grieved for the hardness of the hearts of thy father's house, and thou has longed for their salvation. The Lord will have respect for thy cries, and by his judgments he will cause some of them to see their folly and repent of their sins; but it will be by affliction that they will be saved.
>
> Thou shalt see many days, yea, the Lord will spare thee till thou art satisfied, for thou shalt see thy Redeemer. Thy heart shall rejoice in the great work of the Lord, and no one shall take thy rejoicing from thee. Thou shalt ever remember the great condescension of thy God in permitting thee to accompany my son when the angel delivered the record of the Nephites to his care. Thou hast seen much sorrow because the Lord has taken from thee three of thy children. In this thou art not to be blamed, for He knows thy pure desires to raise up a family, that the name of my son might be blessed. And now, behold,

I say unto thee, that thus [saith] the Lord, if thou wilt believe, thou shalt yet be blessed in this thing and thou shalt bring forth other children, to the joy and satisfaction of thy soul, and to the rejoicing of thy friends. Thou shalt be blessed with understanding, and have power to instruct thy sex, teach thy family righteousness, and thy little ones the way of life, and the holy angels shall watch over thee and thou shalt be saved in the Kingdom of God, even so, Amen.[6]

March 27, 1836 was a glorious day for the members of The Church of Jesus Christ of Latter-day Saints in Kirtland, Ohio, because this was the day of the dedication of their beautiful temple. The new hymn, *The Spirit of God Like a Fire is Burning*, was sung at this dedication, and it was truly appropriate, because the Spirit of God was there in great abundance.

The love of the Saints in Kirtland for their temple was intense. They had built it under much persecution and duress. Sidney Rigdon said in his dedication speech that many of the Saints had wet the walls of the temple with their tears "in the silent shades of night, while they prayed to the God of Heaven to protect them, and stay the unhallowed hands of ruthless spoilers," who said that when the foundation of the temple was laid, "the walls would never be reared."[7]

At this glorious dedication the Prophet Joseph Smith gave the dedicatory prayer and the elders passed the sacrament to the members of the Church.

The Spirit of the Lord was plainly manifested on this special occasion. After the Prophet Joseph Smith "blessed the congregation in the name of the Lord, . . . the assembly dispersed a little past four o'clock, having manifested the most quiet demeanor during the whole exercise."[8]

At "first candle light," the brethren returned for a special meeting. Again the Spirit of the Lord was clearly manifested, as described by the Prophet Joseph Smith in the following words:

> Brother George A. Smith arose and began to prophesy, when a noise was heard like the sound of a rushing mighty wind, which filled the Temple, and all the congregation simultaneously arose, being moved upon by an invisible power; many began to speak in tongues and prophesy; others saw glorious visions; and I [Joseph Smith] beheld the Temple was filled with angels, which fact I declared to the congregation. The people of the neighborhood came running together (hearing an unusual sound within, and seeing a bright light like a piller of fire resting upon the Temple), and were astonished at what was taking place. This continued until the meeting closed at eleven p.m.[9]

On June 20, 1836, less than three months after the dedication of the Kirtland Temple, Emma and Joseph were blessed with another child, whom they named Frederick. The Prophet Joseph Smith was with Emma when this baby was born. They now had three living children—Julia, Joseph III, and little Frederick.

V

Far West

"Oh my affectionate Emma, I want you to remember
that I am a true and faithful friend to you and the
children forever."

—*Joseph Smith*

January 1838 began as a sad New Year for the Saints in
Kirtland. The Prophet Joseph Smith described it as follows:

January, 1838.—A new year dawned upon the
Church in Kirtland in all the bitterness of the spirit
of apostate mobocracy; which continued to rage and

grow hotter and hotter, until Elder Rigdon and myself were obliged to flee from its deadly influence, as did the Apostles and Prophets of old, and as Jesus said, "when they persecute you in one city, flee to another." On the evening of the 12th of January, about ten o'clock, we left Kirtland, on horseback, to escape mob violence, which was about to burst upon us under the color of legal process to cover the hellish designs of our enemies, and to save themselves from the judgment of the law.[1]

We continued our travels during the night, and at eight o'clock on the morning of the 13th, arrived among the brethren in Norton Township, Medina county, Ohio, a distance of sixty miles from Kirtland. Here we tarried about thirty-six hours, when our families arrived; and on the sixteenth we pursued our journey with our families, in covered wagons toward the city of Far West, in Missouri.[2]

When I had arrived within one hundred and twenty miles of Far West, the brethren met me with teams and money to help me forward; and when eight miles from the city, we were met by an escort, viz., Thomas B. Marsh and others, who received us with open arms; and on the 13th of March, with my family and some others I put up at Brother Barnard's for the night. Here we were met by another escort of the brethren from the town, who came to make us welcome to their little Zion.[3]

On the 14th of March, as we were about entering Far West, many of the brethren came out to meet us, who also with open arms welcomed us to their bosoms. We were immediately received under the hospitable roof of Brother George W. Harris, who treated us with all possible kindness, and we refreshed ourselves with much satisfaction, after our long and tedious journey, the brethren bringing in such things as we had need of for our comfort and convenience.[4]

The trip from Kirtland to Far West was hard for Emma. Again she was expecting a baby. Two months after she and Joseph arrived in Far West, she gave birth to another baby boy, Alexander.

Before Emma could regain her strength after the birth of Alexander, some of the fiercest persecutions of the Church took place. The persecutions in Missouri were made worse by bitter apostates who intentionally came to Missouri for the sole purpose of defaming the Prophet and destroying the Church. Mobbings, beatings, burnings, killings, etc., were reenacted in Missouri, until the Saints had to arm themselves for defense.

To add to the misery of the Saints, Lilburn W. Boggs, one of the leaders of the mob in Jackson County, Missouri, who had looked on with approval as he saw the Saints being persecuted, was now the Governor of the state of Missouri. On October 27, 1838, Governor Boggs issued the famous "Extermination Order." It was in the form of a letter to General Clark, which said, "Your orders are, therefore, to hasten your operations and endeavor to reach Richmond, in Ray County, with all possible speed. The Mormons must be treated as enemies and must be exterminated or driven from the state, if necessary for the public good."[5]

The mob evidently knew about the "Extermination Order" before it was issued by Governor Boggs, because they began to encamp at Richmond a day before the order was issued. At this time the mob in Richmond amounted to about 2,000 men, "all ready to fulfill the exterminating order."[6]

On October 30, 1838, the Haun's Mill Massacre occurred. It was a terrible example of mob brutality in which seventeen Saints were killed. Many others were wounded or left homeless.

The day after this horrible massacre, the Prophet Joseph Smith, Sidney Rigdon, Hyrum Smith, Parley P. Pratt, Lyman Wight, Amasa Lyman, and George W. Robison were taken prisoner by Governor Boggs' militia, which was composed of members of the mob. Joseph and his fellow prisoners were taken the next day to the public square in Far West, where they begged their guards to let them see their families before they were taken to Independence, where they were to be put in prison. After much pleading, they were allowed to see their families, but only under heavy guard. In his journal, Joseph described this sad occasion as follows:

> I found my wife and children in tears, who feared we had been shot by those who had sworn to take our lives, and that they would see me no more. When I entered my house, they clung to my gar-

ments, their eyes streaming with tears, while mingled emotions of joy and sorrow were manifested in their countenances.

I requested to have a private interview with them a few minutes, but this privilege was denied me by the guard. I was then obliged to take my departure. Who can realize the feelings which I experienced at that time, to be thus torn from my companion, and leave her surrounded with monsters in the shape of men, and my children, too, not knowing how their wants would be supplied; while I was to be taken far from them in order that my enemies might destroy me when they thought proper to do so.

My partner wept, my children clung to me, until they were thrust from me by the swords of the guards. I felt overwhelmed while I witnessed the scene, and could only recommend them to the care of that God whose kindness had followed me to the present time, and who alone could protect them, and deliver me from the hands of my enemies, and restore me to my family.

After this painful scene I was taken back to the camp . . . with the rest of my brethren.[7]

Joseph Smith and his fellow prisoners were then taken to Independence, Missouri. At this time Joseph recorded in his diary: "We were ushered into a vacant house prepared for our reception, with a floor for our beds and blocks of wood for our pillows."[8] Joseph's thoughts remained with Emma and his children as shown in the following excerpt from a letter he wrote to his "dear and beloved companion":

Independence, Missouri
November 4, 1838

My dear and beloved companion,

I have great anxiety about you and my lovely children. . . . Those little children are subjects of my
meditation continually. Tell them that father is yet
alive. . . . Oh Emma . . . If I do not meet you again
in this life . . . may God grant that . . . we meet in
heaven.[9]

Joseph's anguish on being in prison and his desire to be
with Emma forever is expressed in the following poignant
words: "Oh Emma for God's sake do not forsake me nor the
truth, but remember me. . . . I cannot express my feelings, my
heart is full. Farewell, Oh my kind and affectionate Emma. I
am yours forever."[10]

Emma, true to Joseph, assured him that cruel injustice
could not separate them. They would always be together in
spirit. Emma had suffered much with and for her Prophet husband, and she was willing to suffer more if it were the will of
God. Emma expressed this in the following majestic words:
"The situation in which you are, the walls, the bars, the bolts,
rolling rivers, running streams, rising hills, sinking vallies and
spreading prairies that separate us and the cruel injustice that
first cast you into prison and still holds you there, with many
other considerations, places my feelings far beyond description,
. . . but I still live and am yet willing to suffer more if it is the
will of kind Heaven, that I should for your sake."[11]

Joseph and his fellow prisoners did not remain long in Independence, Missouri, before they were taken to Richmond, Missouri, and placed in prison there. When a letter from Emma reached him in the Richmond prison, he expressed his great appreciation for it in the following words: "I received your letter which I read over and over again, it was a sweet morsal to me. Oh God grant that I may have the privilege of seeing once more my lovely family, in the enjoyment of the sweets of liberty . . . to press them to my bosom and kiss their lovely cheeks would fill my heart with unspeakable gratitude."[12]

Joseph wrote the following letter to Emma from Richmond prison:

Richmond, Missouri
November 12, 1838

My dear Emma,

We are prisoners in chains, and under strong guard for Christ's sake. . . . Tell the children that I am alive and trust I shall come and see them before long. Comfort their hearts all you can, and try to be comforted yourself. . . . Tell little Joseph he must be a good boy; Father loves him with a perfect love, he is the eldest [and] must not hurt those that are smaller than him but comfort them. Tell little Frederick, Father loves him with all his heart; he is a lovely boy. Julia is a lovely little girl; I love her also. She is a promising child; tell her, Father wants her to remember him and be a good girl. . . . Little Alexander is on my mind continually. Oh my affectionate Emma, I want you to remember that I am a true and faithful friend to you, and the children, forever. Oh, may God bless you all.[13]

Eventually Joseph and his fellow prisoners were taken from the prison in Richmond, Missouri, and put in Liberty Jail. Following are excerpts from two letters Joseph wrote to Emma when he was confined in Liberty Jail:

Liberty Jail
March 15, 1839

My Affectionate Wife—

. . . I was glad to see you. No tongue can tell what inexpressible joy it gives a man to see the face of one who has been a friend, after having been inclosed in the walls of a prison for five months. It seems to me my heart will always be more tender after this than ever it was before. . . . For my part I think I never could have felt as I now do if I had not suffered the wrongs which I have suffered. All things shall work together for good to them that love God.[14]

Liberty Jail
March 21, 1839

My dear Emma,

I very well know your trials, and sympathize with you. If God will spare my life once more to have the privilege of taking care of you I will ease your care and endeavor to comfort your heart. I want you to take the best care of the family you can which I believe you will do all you can. I was sorry to learn that Frederick was sick, but I trust he is well again and that you are all well. I want you to try to gain time and write to me a long letter and tell me all you can. . . . and what those little pratlers say that cling around your neck. Do you tell them I am in prison that their lives might be saved.[15]

The prophet's heavy responsibilities, coupled with the many unjust persecutions and imprisonments he suffered, kept him away from his home and family for months at a time. While he was away, Emma had the responsibility of caring for their home and family. This also included many financial responsibilities in providing the necessities of life for their children. She did this by taking boarders into her home.

Emma was a kind, affectionate mother in taking care of her children as she helped them enjoy their childhood. Her son, Joseph III, relates the following incident in which his mother helped him enjoy fishing with the other boys in a stream near his home:

> My mother, to gratify me, procured a little pole and attached a thread thereto, with a bent pin for a hook, and away I marched to the creek. I threw my hook without bait into the water and the little fishes gathered to it as it fell. By some strange chance one became fastened to it and was drawn to the shore. In great excitement I dropped the pole and gathering the

fish in my hands rushed to the house with it, shouting, "I've got one! I've got one!"[16]

We do not know how many times Emma visited Joseph while he was in Liberty Jail, but we do have a record of her visiting him three times. The third recorded visit was on January 21, 1839, a sad one, because after this visit, Emma did not know whether she would ever see her husband again. In a short time she, too, would be one of the exiled Saints driven from the state of Missouri by the cruel "Extermination Order" of Governor Boggs.

VI

Nauvoo

"With what unspeakable delight, and what transports of joy swelled my bosom, when I took by the hand, on that night, my beloved Emma—she that was my wife, even the wife of my youth, and the choice of my heart. . . . Oh what a commingling of thought filled my mind for the moment, again she is here, even in the seventh trouble—undaunted, firm and unwavering—unchangeable, affectionate Emma!"

—Joseph Smith

On February 15, 1839, when one of the last groups of Saints left Missouri and crossed the frozen Mississippi River into Quincy, Illinois, Emma Smith and her children were with them. Under her skirts in two cotton bags,. Emma carried the manuscript for the "Inspired Version" of the Bible on which

Joseph had worked for a long time before his imprisonment. In her arms she carried her two youngest children, Alexander and Frederick. The two older children, Julia and Joseph III, clung to her skirts as she walked across the frozen Mississippi River on the ice that bitter February day.[1]

Emma became the guardian of the manuscript of the "Inspired Version" of the Bible as follows:

> In Far West James Mulholland had charge of Joseph's papers. . . . Aware of the value of Joseph's papers when the storm was breaking, he turned them over to his wife's sister, Anne Scott, concluding that they would be safer with her. Anne made two cloth bags of sufficient size to hold the papers containing the revised scriptures. She sewed bands around the tops long enough to button around her waist. These she carried under the folds of her dress in the daytime and placed under her pillow at night. During the closing days of Far West Anne gave these papers to Emma Smith. They remained in these bags when Emma crossed Missouri and she carried them with her as she walked across the Mississippi River on February 15, 1839.[1]

The kind citizens of Quincy treated the exiled Latter-day Saints with compassion and assisted them in their needs.

Many of the Saints were in the area of Quincy when Emma and her children arrived there. John and Sarah Cleveland, members of the Church who lived about three miles from Quincy, took Emma and her children into their home and treated them with much kindness.

After Emma was settled in the Cleveland home, she wrote to Joseph about her "journey out of the state of Missouri":

> No one but God, knows the reflections of my mind and the feelings of my heart when I left our house and home, and almost all of everything that we possessed excepting our little children, and took my journey out of the state of Missouri, leaving [you] shut up in that lonesome prison.[2]

Emma's most precious possessions were her four little children who clung to her as she walked across the frozen Mississippi River. The anguish she had suffered in losing four babies before Joseph III was born made her four living children even more precious to her. Although she had to leave her home and almost everything she possessed behind her in the state of Missouri, she was thankful that she was able to bring her four little children with her into the freedom of the state of Illinois. But how sad she must have felt for her husband, "shut up in that lonesome prison" in the hostile state of Missouri!

Joseph suffered intensely while he was incarcerated in Liberty Jail. It was here that he wrote Section 122 of the Doctrine and Covenants, which is a great consolation to all those who suffer for the sake of righteousness. It is reminiscent of Joseph's being torn from his wife and children before his incarceration in Liberty Jail. Following is an excerpt from this section:

> If thou art called to pass through tribulation; if thou art in perils among false brethren; if thou art in perils among robbers; if thou art in perils by land or by sea;
>
> If thou art accused with all manner of false accusations; if thine enemies fall upon thee; if they tear thee from the society of thy father and mother and brethren and sisters; and if with a drawn sword thine enemies tear thee from the bosom of thy wife, and of thine offspring, and thine elder son, although but six years of age, shall cling to thy garments, and shall say, My father, my father, why can't you stay with us? O, my father, what are the men going to do with you? and if then he shall be thrust from thee by the sword, and thou be dragged to prison, and thine enemies prowl around thee like wolves for the blood of the lamb; . . . know thou, my son, that all these things shall give thee experience, and shall be for thy good.

The Son of Man hath descended below them all. Art thou greater than he? . . . Fear not what man can do, for God shall be with you forever and ever. (D&C 122:5-9.)

After Joseph and his fellow prisoners had been confined in the Liberty Jail about five months, Joseph obtained a change of venue from Liberty, Clay County, to Gallatin in Daviess County, and then from Gallatin to Columbia in Boone County. It was while they were being taken from Daviess County to Boone County that they were able to make an escape from their unjust imprisonment. On April 22, 1839, they arrived in Quincy, Illinois.[3]

Joseph went immediately to the Cleveland home where Emma and the children were staying. "On arriving at the house where his family was, Emma knew him as he was dismounting from his horse. She met him half way to the gate."[4] One can imagine Emma's joy in suddenly seeing her husband again. The last time she had seen him was when he was in that *loathsome* prison.

Finding a permanent home for the Latter-day Saints to live in Illinois was the next problem facing the Prophet. The citizens in Quincy had been kind to the Saints, but from past experience the Saints knew that this kindness would not last if they remained too long. Religious differences had forced the Saints from city to city and from state to state. Would perse-cution ever end if the Saints went into a land inhabited by other people? The answer was to find a place that was desolate —a wilderness that no one else wanted. Such a place presented itself in a tract of land located about forty miles northwest of Quincy. This was an old trading post called Commerce, which had twelve old dilapidated buildings on it. The area was a swampy, boggy marsh situated in a horseshoe bend of the Mississippi River. Apparently it was a desolate place that no one else wanted, so it was offered to the Prophet Joseph Smith at a very low cost because it had little in its favor as seen through the eyes of an ordinary man. Joseph, however, was a man of vision. He knew that the swamp could be drained and that the area could become a place for a beautiful city. The horseshoe bend in the river provided a picturesque setting for a city, and convenient water transportation would be a great advantage in getting materials for building.

Joseph and the other Church authorities purchased the land and the old trading post buildings in the area of Commerce. After the purchase, the Saints began moving from Quincy to Commerce. Emma and Joseph and their children moved into an old two-story log building which they called their "Homestead." Other Saints moved into other old buildings on this trading post or wherever they could find shelter while they waited for the purchased land to be divided into building lots for them to again build homes for their families.

The swampy land in the area of Commerce was infested with mosquitoes, which caused many of the Saints to become ill with malarial fever. They called this fever the "ague." This terrible disease caused many of the saints to suffer; some died from it. The Prophet Joseph Smith also became ill with the ague. Emma was like an angel of mercy as she administered to the physical and spiritual needs of those who were sick and dying in her "Homestead" home and the area surrounding it. On page 56 is a picture of a painting by Theodore Gorka, titled *Emma Smith, the Elect Lady of the Restoration.* This painting shows Emma taking care of the sick and dying Latter-day Saints during the plague of malarial fever which the Saints suffered during the summer of 1839. This painting was displayed in the LDS Visitors' Center in Salt Lake City for a number of years. The following explanation accompanied it: "Emma was termed the 'Ministering Angel' by her patients. The figure of Emma is placed centrally in the composition, a wagon wheel placed just behind her head, reinforcing the artist's idea of Emma acting as the hub of a wheel radiating compassion to all those around her."

Emma Smith, the Elect Lady of the Restoration

After the Prophet recovered from the ague, he decided to go to Washington, D.C. to lay before the Congress of the United States the grievances of the Saints and petition the Congress for redress for the wrongs inflicted upon them in Missouri. Inasmuch as the Latter-day Saints had been driven from one state to another, it seemed that the restitution for their losses in Missouri might rightfully involve the federal government. With the Governor and most of the people in Missouri prejudiced against the Latter-day Saints, it was impossible for them to get payment for the property they had to leave in Missouri—their homes they had built and the lands they had purchased. Much of the land they had bought direct-ly from the federal government. Therefore, the Prophet Joseph Smith, accompanied by Sidney Rigdon, Elias Higbee and Porter Rockwell, left Commerce on October 29, 1839, to go to Washington, D.C. to see if they could get some redress for the wrongs they had suffered when they were driven from Missouri to Illinois under Governor Boggs' cruel "Extermina-tion Order."[5]

During their stay in Washington, D.C., the Prophet Joseph Smith had a personal interview with President Martin Van Buren. After listening to their grievances, President Van Buren said: "Gentlemen, your cause is just, but I can do nothing for you. . . If I take up for you, I shall lose the vote of Missouri."[6]

After their interview with President Van Buren, Joseph and his friends decided to return to their homes in Commerce. They knew then that they could not expect any help from the federal government. Apparently political expediency meant more to President Van Buren than did the preservation of human rights.

On January 20, 1840 Joseph wrote a letter to Emma in which he said:

> "I am making all haste to arrange my business to start home. I feel very anxious to see you all once more. . . . The time seems long that I am deprived of your society. . . . I pray God to spare you all until I get home. My dear Emma, my heart is intwined around you and those little ones."[7]

On June 13, 1840, Emma gave birth to another child, whom Joseph and Emma named Don Carlos. He was a beautiful baby, and he brought Emma much joy. She saw him develop into a happy little toddler, but when he was just fourteen months old, he died. Again Emma was stricken with grief. Her loss of three babies at birth brought her great sorrow, but losing little Don Carlos when he was fourteen months old was almost more than Emma could bear. She carried her grief for the loss of little Don Carlos until almost the day she died. Shortly before her death she had a dream of seeing little Don Carlos again. The details of this dream are related in the last chapter of this book.

After Joseph returned from Washington, D.C., the building of a beautiful Latter-day Saint city in Illinois on the site of Commerce progressed rapidly. The timber along the river line was removed in order to drain the area and abate the mosquitoes. Then the city was laid out in an orderly fashion.

This city which Joseph planned for the Saints grew into the place he had visualized. In the process of building, its name was changed from Commerce to Nauvoo, a Hebrew word meaning "a beautiful place or situation."

Joseph knew that if the Saints were to be preserved in their human rights, it would have to be done on a local basis. Accordingly, he drew up a charter for the city of Nauvoo, which was granted by the Illinois State Legislature. Because it was a very liberal charter, it granted Nauvoo many rights and privileges. The charter permitted the city of Nauvoo to have its own military force, called the Nauvoo Legion. Thomas Carlin, the Governor of Illinois, commissioned the Prophet Joseph Smith as the first in command of the Nauvoo Legion, giving him the title of Lieutenant General.

For about two years the Prophet had gone without being arrested for his previous escape. Then, on June 5, 1841, when Joseph Smith was returning to Nauvoo from Quincy, where he had gone to say goodbye to some missionaries who were leaving to go to the Eastern States, he was arrested by Sheriff King of Missouri. He was charged with being a fugitive from justice. After the arrest, Joseph went immediately to Quincy and obtained a writ of *habeas corpus*. Judge Stephen A. Douglas, who was in Quincy at that time, made arrangements for a hearing of the writ in Monmouth, Warren County, Illinois, on the following Tuesday.[8]

On Tuesday, June 8, Joseph recorded in his diary:

"Arrived at Monmouth and procured breakfast at the tavern; found great excitement prevailing in the public mind, and great curiosity was manifested by the citizens who were extremely anxious to obtain a sight of the Prophet, expecting to see me in chains."[9]

Wednesday, June 9, was the day of the trial. The Prophet Joseph Smith obtained the services of a friendly attorney, O. H. Browning, Esq., to defend him at the trial. Following is an excerpt from the Nauvoo newspaper, *The Times and Seasons*, concerning Joseph's trial at Monmouth:

[O. H. Browning, Esq.] sympathized with us in our afflictions. . . . His was not an effort of a lawyer anxious to earn his fee, but the pure and patriotic feelings of Christian benevolence, and a sense of justice and of right. While he was answering the monstrous and ridiculous arguments urged by the opposing counsel, that Joseph Smith might go to Missouri and have his trial; he stated the circumstances of our being driven from that State, and feelingly and empathically pointed out the impossibility of our obtaining justice there. There we were forbidden to enter in consequences of the order of the Executive, and that injustice and cruelties of the most barbarous and atrocious character had been practiced upon us, until the streams of Missouri had run with blood, and that he had seen women and children, barefoot and houseless crossing the Mississippi to seek refuge from ruthless mobs. He concluded his remarks by saying that to tell us to go to Missouri for a trial was adding insult to injury; and then he said: "Great God! have I not seen it? Yes, my eyes have beheld the blood-stained traces of innocent women and children, in the drear winter, who had traveled hundreds of miles barefoot, through frost and snow, to seek a refuge from their savage pursuers. 'Twas a scene of horror sufficient to enlist sympathy from an adamantine heart. And shall this unfortunate man, whom their fury has seen proper to select for sacrifice, be driven into such a savage land and none dare to enlist in the cause of Justice? If there was no other voice under heaven ever to be heard in this cause, gladly would I stand alone, and proudly spend my latest breath in defense of an oppressed American citizen."[10]

On Thursday, June 10, 1841, "The court was opened about 8 o'clock a.m. when Judge Douglas delivered his opinion on the case." He ruled that the Missouri writ was dead.[11] Joseph was liberated and discharged about eleven o'clock that morning.[12] In his diary for this date the Prophet Joseph Smith recorded, "Thus have I been once more delivered from the fangs of my cruel persecutors, for which I thank God, my Heavenly Father."[13] Early the next morning Joseph and his friends began their return trip to Nauvoo. Joseph Smith's diary states that when they arrived in Nauvoo he "was met by the acclamation of the Saints."[14]

On February 7, 1842, Emma gave birth to a little baby boy which did not survive its birth.[15] Again she was overcome with grief. Five months before this stillborn birth, Emma's little toddler, Don Carlos, died. This caused her much sorrow. She had anxiously looked forward to the birth of this baby, but when it arrived it was a "silent baby," so it could not relieve the anguish she felt in losing her little Don Carlos, as well as this baby.

Joseph had great empathy for Emma. He thought that if he could borrow a living baby, perhaps for only a few hours a day, it might help Emma recover from her sorrow in the stillborn loss. One of Emma's friends, Mrs. McIntyre, had recently given birth to twin babies. Joseph thought that if he could borrow one of Mrs. McIntyre's babies for the day and bring it back at night, it would be a comfort to Emma. So Joseph asked Mrs. McIntyre if he could borrow one of her twins until Emma could be comforted. Mrs. McIntyre consented to let Emma take one of her babies during the day, but Joseph had to promise that he would bring it home each night. Joseph agreed to do this. He called for the baby, little Mary, each morning and brought her home each night at approximately the same time. One evening, however, Joseph did not bring the baby home at the usual time, and Mrs. McIntyre went to see what was the matter; "there sat the Prophet with the baby wrapped up in a little silk quilt. He was trotting it on his knee, and singing to it to get it quiet before starting out, as it was fretting." The next morning when Joseph came to borrow the baby, Mrs. McIntyre gave him the other twin, Sarah, by mistake. Joseph shook his head and said, "This is not my little Mary." The mother then took little Mary from the cradle and gave her to Joseph. Joseph continued this program of borrowing the baby until Emma could be comforted.[16]

On March 17, 1842, the Prophet Joseph Smith organized the Female Relief Society of Nauvoo. His wife, Emma, was "elected" as the first president of this organization, with Elizabeth Ann Whitney and Sarah M. Cleveland as her counselors. In his diary of this day the Prophet Joseph Smith wrote:

> I gave much instruction, read in the New Testament, and book of Doctrine and Covenants, concerning the Elect Lady, and showed that the elect meant to be elected to a certain work, etc., and that the revelation was then fulfilled by Sister Emma's election to the Presidency of the [Relief] Society. . . . Emma was blessed, and her counselors were ordained by Elder John Taylor.[17]

On April 28, 1842, the Prophet Joseph Smith met with the Relief Society and delivered a long address. He quoted a great deal from the thirteenth chapter of First Corinthians in explaining the meaning of the word "charity." The motto of the Relief Society is "Charity Never Faileth." Joseph said:

This is a charitable Society, and according to your natures; it is natural for females to have feelings of charity and benevolence. You are now placed in a situation in which you can act according to those sympathies which God has planted in your bosoms.

If you live up to these principles, how great and glorious will be your reward in the celestial kingdom! If you live up to your privileges, the angels cannot be restrained from being your associates.[18]

You will receive instructions through the order of the Priesthood which God has established, through the medium of those appointed to lead, guide and direct the affairs of the Church in this last dispensation; and I now turn the key in your behalf in the name of the Lord, and this Society shall rejoice, and knowledge and intelligence shall flow down from this time henceforth; this is the beginning of better days to the poor and needy, who shall be made to rejoice and pour forth blessings on your heads.[19]

On May 22, 1842, the Prophet Joseph Smith was at his home looking through various newspapers, when, to his amazement, he saw an article published in the *Quincy Whig*, which said that Lilburn W. Boggs had been shot by a would-be assassin. It also mentioned a rumor in circulation that Joseph Smith was responsible for the attempted assassination, because when Mr. Boggs was governor of Missouri, he was "in no small degree" instrumental in driving the Mormons from the state of Missouri.[20]

After Ex-governor Boggs recovered from the attempted assassination, he requested Governor Reynolds of Missouri to ask Governor Carlin of Illinois to issue a warrant for the arrest of Joseph Smith as "being an accessory before the fact to an assault with intent to kill made by one Orrin P. Rockwell on Lilburn W. Boggs," on May 6, 1842.[21]

Although the Prophet Joseph Smith was not responsible for the attempted assassination of Ex-governor Boggs, when Joseph found out about the warrant of arrest, he went into seclusion, because he knew from bitter experience that if he were arrested and dragged back to Missouri, there would be no justice for him. Joseph hid himself on a small island in the Mississippi River between Nauvoo and Zarahemla, while his friends sought the legal advice of Judge Butterfield, the United States attorney for the District of Illinois. Only Joseph's very best friends knew where he was, and they came at night to see him so that they would not disclose his hiding place.

Emma came to see Joseph as often as she could while he was secluded on the island. Following is a beautiful tribute Joseph wrote to Emma after one of her visits:

How glorious were my feelings when I met that faithful and friendly band, on the night of the

eleventh, on Thursday, on the island at the mouth of
the slough, between Zarahemla and Nauvoo: with
what unspeakable delight, and what transports of joy
swelled my bosom, when I took by the hand, on that
night, my beloved Emma—she that was my wife, even
the wife of my youth, and the choice of my heart.
Many were the reverberations of my mind when I
contemplated for a moment the many scenes we had
been called to pass through, the fatigues and the toils,
the sorrows and sufferings, and the joys and consola-
tions, from time to time, which had strewed our
paths and crowned our board. Oh what a commingling of thought filled my mind for the moment, again
she is here, even in the seventh trouble—undaunted,
firm, and unwavering—unchangeable, affectionate
Emma![22]

Emma had to be very cautious when she came to see
Joseph in his seclusion. If one of Joseph's enemies found him
by following her, he could kidnap Joseph and carry him off to
his enemies in Missouri. On August 13, 1842, Joseph recorded the following in his diary:

I had sent a request to Emma to come to see me,
and she concluded to start in the carriage, but while
it was preparing, it attracted the attention of the
sheriff, who kept a close watch of all movements. To
avoid suspicion, Emma walked to Sister Durphy's
and waited the arrival of the carriage which passed off
down the river with William Clayton and Lorin Walker,
with raised curtains, receiving Emma by the way,
without any discovery by the sheriff; when about four

miles down the river, the carriage turned on the prairie and passing around the city, turned into the timber opposite Wiggan's farm, when Emma alighted and walked to Brother Sayers', and the carriage returned. I was in good spirits, although somewhat afflicted in body, and was much rejoiced to meet my dear wife once more.[23]

An excerpt from a letter Joseph wrote to Emma on August 16, 1842, expresses his appreciation for two of her "interesting and consoling visits":

My dear Emma:—I embrace this opportunity to express to you some of my feelings this morning. First of all, I take the liberty to tender to you my sincere thanks for the two interesting and consoling visits that you have made me during my almost exiled situation. Tongue cannot express the gratitude of my heart, for the warm and true-hearted friendship you have manifested in these things towards me.[24]

On August 17, 1842, Joseph Smith recorded in his diary:

"I walked out into the woods for exercise in company with Brother Derby where we were accidentally discovered by a young man. We asked him various questions concerning the public feeling and situation of matters around, to all which he answered promptly. On being requested not to make it known where we were, he promised faithfully he would not."[25]

Joseph also recorded the following in his diary on this same day:

> "Several rumors were afloat in the city, intimating that my retreat had been discovered, and that it was no longer safe for me to remain at Brother Sayers'; consequently Emma came to see me at night, and informed me of the report. It was considered wisdom that I should remove immediately, and accordingly I departed in company with Emma and Brother Derby, and went to Carlos Granger's, who lived in the north-east part of the city. Here we were kindly received and well treated."[26]

While Joseph was in seclusion, he missed his children. His love for them is evident in what he wrote in his diary on September 9, 1842: "I accompanied the brethren and Emma to my house, remaining there a few minutes to offer a blessing upon the heads of my sleeping children."[27]

After remaining in seclusion for some time at the home of Carlos Granger, Joseph's friends took him to his own home so he could live with his family again. Only his closest friends knew that he was secluded in his own home in Nauvoo. Others thought that he had gone to Washington, others that he had gone to Europe; and some thought that he might be secluded somewhere in the city of Nauvoo.[28]

Emma did not keep a diary, but her love and concern for her husband and her people is expressed in letters she has written. On August 17, 1842, she wrote a long letter to

Governor Carlin, "pleading the cause of the Prophet and the people of Nauvoo."[29]

On August 19, 1842, Joseph made the following entry in his diary:

> William Clayton presented Emma's letter of the 17th to Governor Carlin at Quincy, in presence of Judge Ralston. The governor read the letter with much attention, apparently; and when he got through, he passed high encomiums on Emma Smith, and expressed astonishment at the judgment and talent manifest in the manner of her address. He presented the letter to Judge Ralston, requesting him to read it. Governor Carlin then proceeded to reiterate the same language as on a former occasion, viz., that he was satisfied there was "no excitement anywhere but in Nauvoo, amongst the 'Mormons' themselves;" all was quiet, and no apprehension of trouble in other places, so far as he was able to ascertain.[30]

While Joseph was home again, but in semiseclusion, Emma became very ill. The following entries from Joseph's diary at this time show his deep concern for her:

> Thursday, 29—This day Emma began to be sick with fever; consequently I kept in the house with her all day.
> Friday, 30—Emma is no better. I was with her all day.
> Monday, 3—Emma was a little better. I was with her all day.
> Tuesday, 4—Emma is very sick again. I attended with her all the day.

Wednesday, 5—My dear Emma was worse. Many fears were entertained that she would not recover . . . Thursday, 6—Emma is better; and although it is the day on which she generally grows worse, yet she appears considerably easier. May the Lord speedily raise her to the bosom of her family, that the heart of His servant may be comforted again. Amen.[31]

While Joseph was still in semiseclusion, his friends sought the legal advice of Judge Butterfield, the United States Attorney for the district of Illinois. After Joseph's friends presented the facts of Joseph's warrant of arrest, Judge Butterfield issued a legal opinion very much in favor of the Prophet's being set free if he were arrested on the Missouri warrant. According to Judge Butterfield, the Prophet Joseph Smith would only have to prove that he was *not* in the State of Missouri at the time of the crime—the attempted assassination of Ex-Governor Boggs. This would prove that he did not flee from justice as the warrant of arrest claimed.

After Judge Butterfield's encouraging legal opinion, the Prophet Joseph Smith came out of seclusion and began to live a normal life in the city of Nauvoo. He took advantage of his new freedom by riding in his carriage with Emma and their children. His diary records:

Monday, 31—I rode out to my farm with my children, and did not return until after dark.
Tuesday, Nov. 1, 1842—I rode with Emma to the Temple for the benefit of her health. She is rapidly gaining.
Thursday, 3—Rode out with Emma to the Temple.[32]

On December 13, 1842, Judge Butterfield, accompanied by Dr. Richards, Hyrum Smith, Elder Sherwood and Elder Clayton, went to Springfield, Illinois, and called upon the newly-elected Governor, Thomas Ford, and presented him with an affidavit that Joseph "was in Illinois on the 6th of May . . . and consequently he could not have been concerned in the attempted assassination of Ex-Governor Boggs." They also presented "a petition to Governor Ford to revoke the writ and proclamation of Governor Carlin" for Joseph's arrest.[33]

Judge Butterfield's legal opinion was correct. The Springfield court decided the case in Joseph Smith's favor, and on January 5, 1843, Joseph was "discharged from his arrest."[34] On January 10, in Nauvoo, there was great rejoicing among the Saints because of the Prophet's legal release from oppression.[35]

While the Latter-day Saints were building the beautiful city of Nauvoo, they were also building a large beautiful house for Joseph Smith and his family. They called it the "Mansion House." It had plenty of room for Joseph Smith's family and also plenty of room for guests and boarders. Joseph and his family moved into the "Mansion House" on August 31, 1843.

The Christmas of 1843 was a happy time for Emma and Joseph and their children. They were now living in their beautiful new Mansion House. Joseph recorded this joyful Christmas in his diary:

This morning, about one o'clock, I was aroused by an English sister, Lettice Rushton, widow of Richard Rushton, Senior, (who, ten years ago, lost her sight,) accompanied by three of her sons, with their wives and her two daughters, with their husbands, and several of her neighbors, singing, "Mortals, awake! with angels join," etc., which caused a thrill of pleasure to run through my soul. All of my family and boarders arose to hear the serenade, and I felt to thank my Heavenly Father for their visit, and blessed them in the name of the Lord. They also visited my brother Hyrum, who was awakened from his sleep. He arose and went out of doors. He shook hands with and blessed each one of them in the name of the Lord, and said that he thought at first that a cohort of angels had come to visit him, it was such heavenly music to him.

At home all day. About noon, gave counsel to some brethren who called on me from Morley Settlement, and told them to keep law on their side, and they would come out well enough.

At two o'clock, about fifty couples sat down at my table to dine. While I was eating, my scribe called, requesting me to solemnize the marriage of his brother, Dr. Levi Richards, and Sara Griffiths; but as I could not leave, I referred him to President Brigham Young, who married them.

A large party supped at my house, and spent the evening in music, dancing, etc., in a most cheerful and friendly manner.[36]

The Mansion House was a huge building, containing twenty-two rooms. It was first planned as a residence for the Prophet's family, but later because so many people took advantage of Joseph's and Emma's generous hospitality, it was decided that it should function as a hotel.

Emma went to St. Louis, Missouri, to purchase furniture and other equipment needed for the Mansion House to function as a hotel. While she was gone, Joseph let his friend, Porter Rockwell, set up a bar in the Mansion House. When Emma arrived home she was surprised and disappointed at what she saw. The most authentic account of Emma's reaction to what she saw is best told by her son, Joseph III, as follows:

> When she returned Mother found installed in the keeping room of the hotel—that is to say, the main room where the guests assembled and where they were received upon arrival—a bar, with counter, shelves, bottles, glasses, and other paraphernalia customary for a fully equipped tavern bar, and Porter Rockwell in charge as tender.
>
> She was very much surprised and disturbed over this arrangement, but said nothing for a while. A few hours later, as I met her in the hall between the dining room and the front room, she asked me where Father was. I told her he was in the front room. She asked, "Is anyone else there?" "Yes," I answered, "quite a number."
>
> Then she told me to go and tell him she wished to see him. I obeyed, and returned with him to the

hall where Mother awaited him. "Joseph," she asked, "what is the meaning of that bar in this house?"

He told her of Porter's arrival and that a place was being prepared for him just across the street, where he would run a barber shop with a bar in connection, explaining that the bar in the hotel was only a temporary arrangement until the building referred to could be finished and ready for occupancy.

There was no excitement or anger in Mother's voice nor in what she said as she replied, but there was distinctness and earnestness I have never forgotten, and which had its effect upon Father as well.

"How does it look," she asked, "for the spiritual head of a religious body to be keeping a hotel in which is a room fitted out as a liquor-selling establishment?"

He reminded her that all taverns had their bars at which liquor was sold or dispensed—which was true at that day—and again urged that it was only for a time and was being done for Porter's benefit, explaining that since Porter had been compelled to leave his own home and had, in a measure, been made a scapegoat for charges that had been made against the two of them, he felt obligated to help him.

Mother's reply came emphatically clear, though uttered quietly: "Well, Joseph, the furniture and other goods I have purchased for the house will come, and you can have some other person look after things here. As for me, I will take my children and go across to the old house and stay there, for I will not have them raised up under such conditions as this arrangement imposes upon us, nor have them mingle with the kind of men who frequent such a place. You are at liberty to make your choice; either that bar goes out of the house, or we will!"

It did not take Father long to make the choice, for he replied immediately, "Very well, Emma; I will have it removed at once"—and he did.

The disagreement mentioned above is the only one I ever heard, or heard of, as occurring between my father and my mother. It has been charged by certain ones advocating plural marriage that she was a thorn in his side, opposing his policies, and leading him an ill life. This is absolutely not true. I was old enough at the time to know what was going on around me, and was closely associated with both my parents. The sleeping room I shared with my brothers was never more than a door away from where Father and Mother slept. Because of the great love and concern Mother had for her children she never wanted us far from her, in order that she might be on hand to take care of us herself in case of necessity. So, I am sure that if there ever were angry words between my parents I should have known it, and I can truthfully state that nothing of the kind ever occurred. Father was a kindly man, and emphatically a home-loving one, whose wife and children were very dear to him and who was, in turn, loved and respected by them.

Hence it came about that the bar which was so distasteful to Mother was promptly removed from the Nauvoo Mansion, and she became its first landlady.[37]

Joseph and Emma had been married sixteen years when they moved into the Mansion House. The spacious Mansion House, with its beauty and comfort and security, was a striking contrast to the homes they had lived in during the first sixteen years of their married life.

"Gentiles" came from far and near to visit Joseph and Emma in their Mansion House. For example, in April 1844, Josiah Quincy[38] visited Joseph and Emma in the Mansion House and commented on Joseph as being "a remarkable individual" and "a fine-looking man." Emma was also regarded as an outstanding person.

The ceremonial life of the city of Nauvoo was enhanced by the Nauvoo Legion. To celebrate special events Emma would dignify the occasion by riding a horse beside her Lieutenant-General husband in the Nauvoo Legion parades. Emma's son, Joseph III, said, "On such occasions my mother rode the black horse, Charlie. She was a splendid horsewoman and made an excellent appearance upon that magnificent animal."[39]

Emma was a gracious "First Lady" in the Mansion House, where she and Joseph entertained distinguished visitors.

"Marriage is Ordained of God"

And again, verily I say unto you, that whoso
forbiddeth to marry is not ordained of God, for
marriage is ordained of God unto man.

Wherefore, it is lawful that he should have one wife,
and they twain shall be one flesh, and all this that
the earth might answer the end of its creation.

—D&C 49:15-16

*E*mma was able to bear all things for her husband and with
her husband—except one thing—plural marriage. Emma apparently loved her husband too much to be able to share him
with other women. Jealousy is usually considered an undesir-
able trait of character, but Emma's jealousy was perhaps a

jealousy like God's. In Exodus 20:3-5, in the Old Testament God says: "Thou shalt have no other gods before me. Thou shalt not make unto thee any graven image, or any likeness of anything that is in the heaven above, or that is in the earth beneath, or that is in the water under the earth; thou shalt not bow down thyself to them, nor serve them; for I the Lord thy God am a jealous God." Because God loves us so much, He is a jealous God. He does not want us to share our love with other "Gods." In a like manner, Emma did not want to share Joseph's love with other women.

Emma was the Prophet's strongest supporter, save only on the sensitive issue of the plurality of wives. Warmly affectionate, she was a woman of intelligence and spirit. When Joseph was in trouble, she defended him tenaciously. When he was ill, she nursed and comforted him. When he did something of note, she was in the front rank of his admirers. When he was disheartened, she was the first to give him encouragement.

These qualities were not lost on Joseph. He loved Emma as no one else. To him, she was the "Elect Lady." She had endured every privation with stoic calm. She had shown a remarkable resiliency in the face of misfortune. Their marital trail was marked by the graves of four infants. She had experienced the terror of seeing her husband beaten, tarred and feathered and threatened with death. She had endured the trauma of seeing him jailed in filthy prisons, surrounded by vicious men. These and other difficulties she faced without complaint as being the common lot of the wife of an uncommon man.

But the thought of sharing her husband with other women was an extremity Emma was not prepared to face.[1]

[Joseph] was forced to weigh his great love for Emma against his resolve to fulfill God's commandment. Had he not loved Emma so deeply, the introduction of plural marriage would not have been so difficult for him.[2]

Ivan J. Barrett, in his book *Joseph and the Restoration*, explains:

At the time this revelation was given (1831), Joseph, engaged in translating or revising the Bible, asked the Lord how he "justified" the "many wives and concubines" of Abraham, Isaac, Jacob, Moses, and David. (D&C 132:1.) The doctrine of celestial marriage or the everlasting covenant of marriage, including plural marriage, was revealed to him. When the communication was first made, the Lord informed Joseph that the time for practicing that principle had not arrived, but would come thereafter; neither should he make a public announcement of it or teach it as a doctrine of the gospel. . . .

During the summer of 1840 an angel of the Lord confronted the Prophet and commanded him, in the name of the Lord, to establish the principle of plural marriage "so long concealed from the knowledge of the Saints and of the world." Joseph Smith well knew that the introduction of this practice would cost him his life. Fearing God rather than man, he put everything on the altar of duty and devotion and began to do as commanded.

To a few trusted friends he taught the principle and led the way himself by taking other women in the bond of eternal marriage.[3]

Buddy Youngreen adds, "Joseph, recognizing the potential dangers in the restored practice, deliberately swore all participating parties to secrecy."[4]

Finally the time came for Emma to hear the written revelation on celestial or plural marriage. Ivan J. Barrett continues:

Until July 12, 1843, the principle of celestial marriage remained an "unwritten law" to the faithful Saints. On the morning of the above date, Hyrum Smith came to his brother Joseph's office in the upper story of the brick store. They conversed on the subject of plural marriage and Hyrum said to Joseph, "If you will write the revelation on Celestial marriage, I will take it and read it to Emma, and I believe I can convince her of the truth, and you will hereafter have peace." The Prophet smiled, "You do not know Emma as well as I do." But Hyrum insisted and further remarked. "The doctrine is so plain, I can convince any reasonable man or woman of its truth, purity and heavenly origin." Joseph agreed to dictate the revelation to his scribe William Clayton, who wrote it down sentence by sentence. After it was written, Clayton read it through slowly and carefully, and the Prophet pronounced it correct. He observed that there was much more on the subject, but what had been dictated would suffice. Hyrum took the revelation and read it to Emma. When he returned, Joseph asked if he had accomplished his objective. Hyrum replied regretfully that he had never taken such a severe lecture in all his life and that Emma remained resentful and angry. Joseph quietly commented, "I told you you did not know Emma as well as I did."[5]

Emma was certainly not alone in her opposition to polygamy. The Federal Government too displayed serious opposition, and studying their reaction may help us understand Emma's reaction against polygamy. Polygamy was practiced by the Latter-day Saints in Utah for many years before it was declared unconstitutional by the United States Supreme Court and discontinued by The Church of Jesus Christ of Latter-day Saints. After the Latter-day Saints had left Nauvoo and were safely settled in Utah, at a conference in Salt Lake City held on August 29, 1852, "the doctrine of plural marriage was announced to the world."[6] This caused a national reaction against polygamy. "By the time of the national political election of 1856, the newly-formed Republican Party had branded polygamy and slavery as the 'twin relics of barbarism.'"[7]

After the practice of polygamy in Utah was announced to the world, many bills and laws were passed by the United States Congress declaring polygamy illegal. On January 6,

1879 the United States Supreme Court decided that polygamy was unconstitutional.[8]

A revelation called the "Manifesto" was issued on October 6, 1890, by Wilford Woodruff, President of The Church of Jesus Christ of Latter-day Saints. It forbids members of the Church to practice polygamy. This official declaration says in part:

> Inasmuch as laws have been enacted by Congress forbidding plural marriages, which laws have been pronounced constitutional by the court of last resort, I hereby declare my intention to submit to those laws, and to use my influence with the members of the Church over which I preside to have them do likewise.
>
> There is nothing in my teachings to the Church or in those of my associates, during the time specified, which can be reasonably construed to inculcate or encourage polygamy; and when any Elder of the Church has used language which appeared to convey any such teaching, he has been promptly reproved. And I now publicly declare that my advice to the Latter-day Saints is to refrain from contracting any marriage forbidden by the law of the land.[9]

The Church of Jesus Christ of Latter-day Saints accepts the following scripture found in the Book of Mormon. In this scripture, Jacob chastises the Nephite men for their unauthorized practice of polygamy, which had "broken the hearts of their tender wives." (Jacob 2:35.)

> For behold, thus saith the Lord: This people begin to wax in iniquity; they understand not the scriptures, for they seek to excuse themselves in committing whoredoms, because of the things which were written concerning David, and Solomon his son.
>
> Behold, David and Solomon truly had many wives and concubines, which thing was abominable before me, saith the Lord. . . .
>
> Wherefore, my brethren, hear me, and hearken to the word of the Lord: For there shall not any man among you have save it be one wife; and concubines he shall have none; . . .
>
> Wherefore, this people shall keep my commandments, saith the Lord of Hosts, or cursed be the land for their sakes.
>
> For if I will, saith the Lord of Hosts, raise up seed unto me, I will command my people; otherwise they shall hearken unto these things. (Jacob 2:23-30.)

The revelation in Section 132 of the Doctrine and Covenants concerning the plurality of wives was given to the Prophet Joseph Smith for two reasons: (1) so that "all things" (Acts 3:21) could be restored when the Gospel of Jesus Christ was restored in these latter days; and (2) so that a righteous seed could be raised up to the Lord, which was done when Utah was colonized and The Church of Jesus Christ of Latter-day Saints was established there.

For if I will, saith the Lord of Hosts, raise up seed unto me, I will command my people; otherwise they shall hearken unto these things. (Jacob 2:30.)

Apparently Emma loved Joseph Smith too much to accept plural marriage, even though it was "ordained of God." She did not live long enough to see plural marriage discontinued by the "Manifesto" of The Church of Jesus Christ of Latter-day Saints.

VIII

"Home They Brought Her Warrior Dead"

> "I am going like a lamb to the slaughter; but I am calm as a summer's morning; I have a conscience void of offense towards God, and towards all men. I shall die innocent, and it shall yet be said of me—He was murdered in cold blood."
>
> —*Joseph Smith*

The Prophet Joseph Smith knew that the practice of plural marriage would "cost him his life."[1] Although it was "ordained of God" when Abraham, Isaac and Jacob practiced it in the right way,[2] it was "abominable" before God when David and Solomon practiced it in the wrong way.[3] When the Lord commanded the Prophet Joseph Smith to restore this "ancient principle," Joseph faced a serious dilemma.

Joseph Smith lived in the nineteenth century—a time when America was, "in the most places, . . . '*strictly moralistic* [emphasis added].' Although a double standard was evident in the differences in punishment meted out for sexual sins, the ideal everywhere was *purity for men as well as women* [emphasis added]. The double standard for sexual behavior, although evident, was not as acceptable then as now: there was little tolerance for the sowing of 'wild oats.' One authority noted that the number of men who responded to the moral idealism of the time and kept themselves pure for marriage was larger in America than elsewhere and larger in the 1830s and 1840s than in probably any previous generation."[4]

Joseph Smith knew that if he announced the practice of plural marriage to the world, it would be viewed as "adultery" and punishment would be "meted out" for this "sexual sin." Therefore, Joseph kept it a secret which he revealed only to some of his closest friends, leaders in the Church whom he felt he could trust.

Joseph was reluctant to reveal plural marriage to his wife, however. He was fearful that Emma would view plural marriage as adultery because of her strict moral standards and her traditional view that all marriages should be monogamous. Joseph "was forced to weigh his great love for Emma against his resolve to fulfill God's commandment. Had he not loved

Emma so deeply, the introduction of plural marriage would not have been so difficult for him."[5]

On June 7, 1844, the secret of plural marriage in Nauvoo was announced to the world in an "abominable" way by a group of apostate men (William Law, his brother Wilson Law, the Higbee brothers, the Foster brothers, and others). These men, who had been excommunicated from the Church, knew that plural marriage was being practiced in secret in the city of Nauvoo by men in high positions in the Church. Some of the men in this apostate group had been leaders in the Church before they were excommunicated. For example, William Law had been the second counselor to the Prophet Joseph Smith. Becoming bitter enemies of the Church after their excommunication, they desired to kill or overthrow the Prophet Joseph Smith and disorganize the city of Nauvoo by repealing the Nauvoo City Charter. Therefore, they established a newspaper called the *Nauvoo Expositor* which "exposed" the practice of plural marriage in Nauvoo. This newspaper also advocated the repeal of the Nauvoo City Charter which they felt granted Nauvoo too much power. "The first and only number of the *Nauvoo Expositor* was published" on Friday, June 7, 1844.[6]

Three days later, on Monday, June 10, 1844, the Prophet Joseph Smith, who was the mayor of Nauvoo at this time, recorded the following in his diary:

I was in the City Council from 10 a.m., to 1:20 p.m., and from 2:20 p.m. to 6:30 p.m. investigating the merits of the *Nauvoo Expositor*, and also the conduct of the Laws, Higbees, Fosters, and others, who have formed a conspiracy for the purpose of destroying my life, and scattering the Saints or driving them from the state.

An ordinance was passed concerning libels. The Council passed an ordinance declaring the *Nauvoo Expositor* a nuisance. I immediately ordered the Marshal to destroy it without delay, and at the same time issued an order to Jonathan Dunham, acting Major-General of the Nauvoo Legion, to assist the Marshal with the Legion, if called upon so to do.

About 8 p.m., the Marshal returned and reported that he had removed the press, type, printed paper, and fixtures into the street, and destroyed them. This was done because of the libelous and slanderous character of the paper, its avowed intention being to destroy the municipality and drive the Saints from the city. The *posse* accompanied by some hundreds of the citizens, returned with the Marshal to the front of the Mansion, when I gave them a short address, and told them they had done right.[7]

After the *Expositor* press had been destroyed, the owners, William Law and his apostate friends, fled to Carthage, where they began to incite the people against the Prophet and the Latter-day Saints in Nauvoo.

The spirit of mobocracy became so terrible in Carthage that Governor Ford, himself, came from Springfield to Carthage to quell the many disturbances and establish order.[8] Governor

Ford was met by William Law and his apostate friends and his newly-acquired mobbish friends, who told the Governor their version of the controversy concerning the destruction of the *Nauvoo Expositor* press and the dangerous powers granted by the Nauvoo City Charter. Trying to be fair to both sides, Governor Ford sent a letter to the mayor of Nauvoo (Joseph Smith) and the city councilmen, asking them to send him one or more representatives to present to him the Nauvoo version of the controversy.

The Prophet Joseph Smith sent John Taylor and Dr. J. M. Bernhisel to Carthage as Governor Ford had requested. Their interview with Governor Ford was very disheartening. They found the Governor surrounded by the Laws, Higbees, Fosters, and others who had already influenced the Governor against Joseph Smith and the city of Nauvoo. John Taylor presented the Nauvoo version of the controversy to Governor Ford and waited for the Governor to give him a letter to take back to Joseph Smith.

After John Taylor and Dr. J. M. Bernhisel returned to Nauvoo with the Governor's letter, Joseph Smith called his brother Hyrum and a number of his dearest friends into the upper room of his house and said:

> Brethren, here is a letter from the Governor which I wish to have read. After it was read through Joseph remarked, "There is no mercy—no mercy here." Hyrum said, "No; just as sure as we fall into

their hands we are dead men." Joseph replied, "Yes; what shall we do, Brother Hyrum?" He replied, "I don't know." All at once Joseph's countenance brightened up and he said, "The way is open. It is clear to my mind what to do. All they want is Hyrum and myself; then tell everybody to go about their business, and not to collect in groups, but to scatter about. There is no doubt they will come here and search for us. Let them search; they will not harm you in person or property. . . . We will cross the river tonight, and go away to the West.[9]

After hurried plans were made for Joseph and Hyrum and a few of their friends to cross the Mississippi River, Joseph Smith made the last entry, a very prophetic one, in his voluminous diary:

"I told Stephen Markham that if I and Hyrum were ever taken again we should be massacred, or I was not a Prophet of God. I want Hyrum to live to avenge my blood, but he is determined not to leave me."[10]

The Prophet's farewell to his family before he crossed the Mississippi River was extremely sad. Emma, expecting another baby, was in the fourth month of her pregnancy. When Joseph came out of his house after his hurried farewell to his family, his friends noticed that his tears were flowing fast, and he held a handkerchief to his face. Followed by his brother Hyrum, he silently got into the boat waiting for him on the bank of the river.

Early the next morning Joseph and his friends were on the Iowa side of the river, where he and Hyrum hid in the house of another friend. Porter Rockwell, who rowed the boat across the river, was instructed to return to Nauvoo that day, get Joseph's and Hyrum's horses, and secretly pass them across the river the following night.

Porter Rockwell did not bring the horses "across the river" to Joseph and Hyrum, but he did bring Reynolds Cahoon, Lorenzo D. Wasson and Hiram Kimball and also a letter from Emma. B. H. Roberts relates the following concerning what happened at this time:

> Emma sent over Orrin P. Rockwell, requesting him to entreat of Joseph to come back. Reynolds Cahoon accompanied him with a letter which Emma had written to the same effect, and she insisted that Cahoon should persuade Joseph to come back and give himself up. When they went over they found Joseph, Hyrum and Willard in a room by themselves, having flour and other provisions on the floor ready for packing.
>
> Reynolds Cahoon informed Joseph what the troops intended to do, and urged upon him to give himself up, inasmuch as the Governor had pledged his faith and the faith of the state to protect him while he underwent a legal and fair trial. Reynolds Cahoon, Lorenzo D. Wasson and Hiram Kimball accused Joseph of cowardice for wishing to leave the people, adding that their property would be destroyed,

and they left without house or home. Like the fable, when the wolves came the shepherd ran from the flock, and left the sheep to be devoured. To which Joseph replied, "If my life is of no value to my friends it is of none to myself."

Joseph said to Rockwell, "What shall I do?" Rockwell replied, "You are the oldest and ought to know best; and as you make your bed, I will lie with you." Joseph then turned to Hyrum, who was talking with Cahoon, and said, "Brother Hyrum, you are the oldest, what shall we do?" Hyrum said, "Let us go back and give ourselves up, and see the thing out." After studying a few moments, Joseph said, "If you go back I will go with you, but we shall be butchered." Hyrum said, "No, no; let us go back and put our trust in God, and we shall not be harmed. The Lord is in it. If we live or have to die, we will be reconciled to our fate."

After a short pause, Joseph told Cahoon to request Captain Daniel C. Davis to have his boat ready at half-past five to cross them over the river.

Joseph and Hyrum then wrote the following letter [to Governor Ford]:

BANK OF THE RIVER MISSISSIPPI,
Sunday, June 23rd, 1844, 2 p.m.

His Excellency Governor Ford:
SIR.—I wrote you a long communication at 12 last night, expressive of my views of your Excellency's communication of yesterday. I thought your letter

rather severe, but one of my friends has just come to me with an explanation from the captain of your *posse* which softened the subject matter of your communication, and gives us greater assurance of protection, and that your Excellency has succeeded in bringing in subjection the spirits which surround your Excellency to some extent. And I declare again the only objection I ever had or ever made on trial by my country at any time, was what I have made in my last letter—on account of assassins, and the reason I have to fear deathly consequences from their hands.

But from the explanation, I now offer to come to you at Carthage on the morrow, as early as shall be convenient for your *posse* to escort us into headquarters, provided we can have a fair trial, not be abused nor have my witnesses abused, and have all things done in due form of law, without partiality, and you may depend on my honor without the show of a great armed force to produce excitement in the minds of the timid.

We will meet your *posse*, if this letter is satisfactory, (if not, inform me) at or near the Mound, at or about two o'clock tomorrow afternoon, which will be as soon as we can get our witnesses and prepare for trial. We shall expect to take our witnesses with us, and not have to wait a subpoena or part at least, so as not to detain the proceedings, although we may want time for counsel.

We remain most respectfully, your excellency's humble servants,

JOSEPH SMITH
HYRUM SMITH[11]

About 4 p.m. Joseph, Hyrum, the Doctor [Willard Richards] and others started back. While walking towards the river, Joseph fell behind with Orrin P. Rockwell. The others shouted to come on. Joseph replied, "It is of no use to hurry, for we are going back to be slaughtered," . . . [Joseph said] that he would like to get the people once more together and talk to them. . . . Rockwell said if that was his wish he would get the people together, and he could talk to them by starlight. . . . They re-crossed the river at half-past five. When they arrived at the Mansion in Nauvoo, Joseph's family surrounded him, and he tarried there all night, giving up the idea of preaching to the Saints by starlight.[12]

Early the next morning, in compliance with the Governor's order, Joseph and about twenty-five of his friends mounted their horses to go to Carthage. Joseph knew that the end of his life was approaching fast. As he passed the beautiful Nauvoo Temple, still under construction, he paused for a moment and looked out upon the beautiful city, built by the industry of the Saints. "This is the loveliest place and the best people under the heavens," he said in admiration. Then in a sad prophetic voice he added, "Little do they know the trials that await them."[13]

At 9:45 that morning, Joseph and his friends arrived at a point about four miles from Carthage, where they were met by a body of about sixty mounted state militiamen sent by the

Governor under the command of Captain Dunn. Captain Dunn presented Joseph with an order from Governor Ford requesting all the state arms in the possession of the Nauvoo Legion, which the Prophet counter-signed. Joseph then turned to his company of men and uttered these prophetic words:

"I am going like a lamb to the slaughter; but I am calm as a summer's morning; I have a conscience void of offense toward God, and toward all men. I shall die innocent, and it shall yet be said of me, 'He was murdered in cold blood!'"[14]

Captain Dunn, fearing that Governor Ford's order to take away the arms of the Nauvoo Legion would meet with great opposition, requested that Joseph Smith and his friends return to Nauvoo with him and help him collect the arms. Joseph complied with this request after writing the following letter and sending it with a messenger to Governor Ford in Carthage:

Four miles West of Carthage Mound,
Hancock County, Illinois,
Monday, 10 o'clock.

His Excellency Governor Ford:
DEAR SIR.—On my way to Carthage to answer your request this morning, I here met Captain Dunn, who has here made known to me your orders to surrender the state arms in possession of the Nauvoo Legion, which command I shall comply with; and that the same may be done properly and without trouble to the state, I shall return with Captain Dunn to Nauvoo, see that the arms are put into his posses-

sion, and shall then return to headquarters in his company, when I shall most cheerfully submit to any requisition of the Governor of our state.

With all due respect to your Excellency, I remain Your obedient servant.

JOSEPH SMITH[15]

The Nauvoo Legion members were infuriated with the Governor's order to give up their arms, but inasmuch as Joseph also requested it and had come back to Nauvoo to carry out the Governor's order, they complied without much opposition.

Before leaving to go back to Carthage, Joseph went to the Mansion House twice to bid Emma and his children fare-well.[16] It was hard for him to leave them. Emma was expecting another baby, and apparently the Prophet knew that it would be a boy, because he had asked her to name the baby David Hyrum after his beloved brother Hyrum, who had stood by him through all the vicissitudes of his trying life, and who now, in the last hours of sorrow, would not leave him, though it meant sacrificing freedom.

Emma asked Joseph to give her a blessing. He told her to write out the best blessing she could think of, and he would sign it when he returned. Emma wrote the following blessing for herself, calling it the desires of her heart:

First of all I would crave as the richest of heaven's blessings would be wisdom from my

Heavenly Father bestowed daily, so that whatever I might do or say, I could not look back at the close of the day with regret, nor neglect the performance of any act that would bring a blessing. I desire the Spirit of God to know and understand myself, I desire a fruitful, active mind, that I may be able to comprehend the designs of God, when revealed through his servants without doubting. I desire the spirit of discernment, which is one of the promised blessings of the Holy Ghost.

I particularly desire wisdom to bring up all the children that are, or may be committed to my charge, in such a manner that they will be useful ornaments in the Kingdom of God, and in a coming day arise up and call me blessed.

I desire prudence that I may not through ambition abuse my body and cause it to become old and care-worn, but that I may wear a cheerful countenance, living to perform all the work that I covenanted to perform in the spirit-world and be a blessing to all who may need aught at my hands.

I desire with all my heart to honor and respect my husband as my head, ever to live in his confidence and by acting in unison with him retain the place which God has given me by his side, and I ask my Heavenly Father, that through humility, I may be enabled to overcome that curse which was pronounced on the daughters of Eve. I desire to see that I may rejoice with them in the blessings which God has in store for all who are willing to be obedient to his requirements. Finally, I desire that whatever may be my lot through life I may be enabled to acknowledge the hand of God in all things.[17]

With a heavy heart, Joseph, still accompanied by his faithful friends, started on his last trip to Carthage. About four miles from Carthage at the point where they had first met Captain Dunn, the party stopped to eat some food they had brought with them. While they were eating and resting, Captain Dunn and his company of mounted militiamen drove up. They were returning to Carthage with the state arms they had taken from the Nauvoo Legion, and they now accompanied Joseph and his friends the remainder of the way, arriving in Carthage about midnight.

Joseph and his friends surrendered themselves to the constable, Mr. Bettisworth, who held the writ against them. They had hoped to be freed immediately with a writ of *habeas corpus*, but the charge against them now was no longer that of destroying the *Expositor* press. The charge had been changed to treason against the state of Illinois for calling out the Nauvoo Legion to protect Nauvoo.[18] Joseph was astounded at this new charge. When the trouble with Carthage arose, Governor Ford had given Joseph Smith authority to protect Nauvoo with the Legion.[19] The liberal Charter of the city of Nauvoo also gave Joseph Smith that right. William Law and his apostate friends, however, had to have a more serious charge to hold Joseph and Hyrum in Carthage. With a charge as serious as "treason," they could not be released on a writ of *habeas corpus*.

Joseph and Hyrum were taken to the Carthage jail and placed under close confinement. In prison, Joseph's heart and thoughts were still with Emma and his children as he wrote:

> Dear Emma, I am very much resigned to my lot, knowing I am justified, and have done the best that could be done. Give my love to the children and all my friends . . . who inquire about me; and as for treason, I know that I have not committed any, and they cannot prove anything of that kind, so you need not have any fears that anything can happen to us on that account. May God bless you all. Amen.[20]

In the Carthage jail, "Joseph bore a powerful testimony to the guards of the divine authenticity of the Book of Mormon, the restoration of the Gospel, the administration of angels, and that the Kingdom of God was again established upon the earth, for the sake of which he was then incarcerated in that prison, and not because he had violated any law of God or man."[21]

> "They retired to rest late. Joseph and Hyrum occupied the only bedstead in the room, while their friends lay side by side on the mattresses on the floor. Dr. Richards sat up writing until his last candle left him in the dark."[22]

Governor Ford had decided to visit Nauvoo, and he had promised to take Joseph with him. But the governor broke his promise by going to Nauvoo the following day and leaving Joseph and Hyrum in jail with a guard made up of their enemies, the Carthage Greys.

That day, June 27, 1844, Joseph was allowed only three of his friends to stay with him in the jail. They were Hyrum, his brother; Dr. Willard Richards, his secretary; and John Taylor, one of his very best friends.

About five o'clock that day, Dr. Richards "glanced an eye by the curtains of the window, and saw about a hundred armed men around the door."[23] This mob encircled the jail, and some of them rushed by the guards up the flight of stairs and tried to burst open the door of the room where the prisoners were confined. Joseph and his friends sprang against the door to hold it as the bullets whizzed up the stairway. One bullet came through the door, hitting Hyrum in the nose, and he fell to the floor exclaiming, "I am a dead man!"[24] As he fell, a bullet fired from a gun on the outside pierced his left side, then another bullet from the door entered his head while a fourth bullet entered his left leg. Hyrum was dead. Bullets poured into the room from every direction; many of them lodged in the ceiling. When Hyrum fell, Joseph exclaimed, "Oh dear, brother Hyrum!"[25]

Joseph knew that the mob would not be satisfied until they had taken his life. Realizing that it might save the lives of his friends, Willard Richards and John Taylor, if he could get out of the room, Joseph turned from the door and sprang into the window. Two bullets fired from the door entered his back; one fired from the outside entered his chest as he fell out of the window and into the hands of his murderers, exclaiming, "Oh Lord, My God!"[26]

John Taylor was wounded in several places as he fell to the floor and rolled under the bed. Dr. Richards, however, remained unhurt. This was a miraculous thing for he was a very large man. His escape literally fulfilled a prophecy made by Joseph Smith about a year before, when Joseph said that the time would come when bullets would fly around Dr. Richards like hail, that he would "see his friends fall" on his right and left, but there would "not be a hole in his garment."[27]

When Joseph fell out of the window a cry went up, "He's leaped the window!" and "the mob on the stairs and in the entry ran out." Dr. Richards then took the wounded John Taylor under his arm and carried him across the hall into an inner dungeon room for safety. While Dr. Richards and John Taylor were in this inner prison room, the mob rushed up the stairs again, but they found only the dead body of Hyrum. Then a loud cry of, "The Mormons are coming!" was heard, which caused the whole murderous mob to flee into the woods.[28]

It was most fortunate that the calm and competent Dr. Richards was left unhurt to take care of his wounded friend, John Taylor, and to arrange to have the bodies of Joseph and Hyrum returned to Nauvoo.

When Dr. Richards neared the city of Nauvoo with the bodies, he was met by thousands of people of the Church who mourned the deaths of their Prophet and Patriarch. An assemblage of about eight or ten thousand people gathered to hear Dr. Richards address them. In spite of their great sorrow, the wise Dr. Richards warned the people to keep the peace. He said that he had pledged his life and honor for their good conduct. Then he told the people to trust to the laws of the land to avenge these murders, and if that failed they could call upon God for vengeance; but at all costs they must keep the peace.

> "The people with one united voice resolved to trust to the law for a remedy of such a high-handed assassination, and when that failed, to call upon God to avenge them of their wrongs. . . ."
>
> "When the bodies of Joseph and Hyrum arrived at the Mansion, the doors were closed immediately. The people were told to go quietly home, and the bodies would be viewed the next morning at eight o'clock."[29]

Alfred Lord Tennyson, the "Poet Laureate" of England, was one of the most famous English poets of the nineteenth century. He lived at the same time as the Prophet Joseph Smith. He was called "the voice of the times," because he could express the feelings of the people of the nineteenth century, with great empathy. During the nineteenth century, the death of a loved one was the cause of the greatest grief. Usually the first reaction to such a death was a silence too deep for expression. The following poem by Tennyson illustrates this emotion.

HOME THEY BROUGHT HER WARRIOR DEAD

Home they brought her warrior dead:
　　She nor swoon'd, nor utter'd cry:
All her maidens, watching, said,
　　"She must weep, or she will die."

Then they praised him, soft and low,
　　Call'd him worthy to be loved,
Truest friend and noblest foe;
　　Yet she neither spoke nor moved.

Stole a maiden from her place,
　　Lightly to the warrior stept,
Took the face-cloth from the face;
　　Yet she neither moved nor wept.

Rose a nurse of ninety years,
　　Set his child upon her knee;
Like summer tempest came her tears—
　　"Sweet my child, I live for thee."
　　—Alfred Lord Tennyson[30]

　　No one but Emma herself knew how Emma felt when they brought the dead body of her prophet husband home to her. Perhaps she felt as the mother in the above poem felt when the dead body of her warrior husband was brought home to her. The grief of the mother in Tennyson's poem was so intense it could only be expressed in the anguish of deep silence that was typical of the nineteenth century. Only the ninety-year-old nurse, who had lived long enough to experience the fullness of life, knew what the mother needed to assuage her grief. She needed something to live for. When the elderly nurse "set his child upon her knee," the anguish of grief was broken, and the mother's tears flowed "like a summer's tempest." The warrior's widow knew then that in her child, she had her husband again.

We do not know how Emma felt immediately after they brought the dead body of her "spiritual warrior" home to her, but we do know how she treasured her children, both the living ones and the dead ones. Her living children could give her the consolation she needed to carry on after the death of her beloved husband. In her children she could have her husband with her always. At the time of the death of the Prophet Joseph Smith, Emma had four living children, and she was expecting another child in less than five months.

Joseph Smith was truly a "spiritual warrior" as shown by the following tribute to him found in Section 135 of the Doctrine and Covenants:

> Joseph Smith, the Prophet and Seer of the Lord, has done more, save Jesus only, for the salvation of men in this world, than any other man that ever lived in it. In the short space of twenty years, he has brought forth the Book of Mormon, which he translated by the gift and power of God, and has been the means of publishing it on two continents; has sent the fulness of the everlasting gospel, which it

contained, to the four quarters of the earth; has brought forth the revelations and commandments which compose this book of Doctrine and Covenants, and many other wise documents and instructions for the benefit of the children of men; gathered many thousands of the Latter-day Saints, founded a great city, and left a fame and name that cannot be slain. He lived great, and he died great in the eyes of God and his people; and like most of the Lord's anointed in ancient times, has sealed his mission and his works with his own blood; and so has his brother Hyrum. In life they were not divided, and in death they were not separated! (D&C 135:3.)

After the bodies of Joseph and Hyrum were prepared for burial, Emma was brought in to view her husband. She "fell forward to the Prophet's face," and kissing him sobbed, "Joseph, speak to me once more."[31] "Thinking to comfort her, someone said, 'this affliction would be to her a crown.' Looking up with tears streaming down her cheeks, Emma replied, 'My husband was my crown.'"[32]

Emma was carried to her room in a state of insensibility, and Joseph's oldest son, Joseph III, then eleven years of age, came to see his father and dropped on his knees before him. Putting his warm, youthful cheek against his father's cold one, he mourned, "Oh my father! My father!"[33]

After Emma and the immediate families of Joseph and Hyrum had viewed the bodies, close friends and relatives were permitted to view them. Each body was put in a coffin. The outside of each coffin was covered with black velvet, and the inside of each coffin was lined with white chambric. Each coffin was then put in a larger box made of rough pine wood.[34]

The next morning the Saints in Nauvoo were permitted to view the bodies. From eight a.m. to five p.m., a living stream of people filed past the coffins. At five o'clock the people of the city were asked to leave so that the families could take their last farewells.[35]

The coffins were then taken out of the boxes into the little bedroom in the northeast corner of the Mansion, and there concealed and the doors locked. Bags of sand were then placed in each end of the boxes, which were nailed up, and a mock funeral took place, the boxes being put into a hearse and driven to the graveyard by William D. Huntington, and there deposited in a grave with the usual ceremonies.

This was done to prevent enemies of the martyred Prophet and Patriarch getting possession of the bodies, as they threatened they would do. As the hearse passed the meeting ground accompanied by a few men, William W. Phelps was preaching the funeral sermon.

About midnight the coffins containing the bodies were taken from the Mansion by Dimick B. Huntington, Edward Hunter, William D. Huntington, William Marks, Jonathan H. Holmes, Gilbert Goldsmith, Alpheus Cutler, Lorenzo D. Wasson, and

Philip B. Lewis, preceded by James Emmitt as guard with his musket.

They went through the garden, round by the pump, and were conveyed to the Nauvoo house, which was then built to the first joists of the basement, and buried in the basement story.

After the bodies were interred, and the ground smoothed off as it was before, and chips of wood and stone and other rubbish thrown over, so as to make it appear like the rest of the ground around the graves, a most terrific shower of rain, accompanied with thunder and lightning, occurred, and obliterated all traces of the fact that the earth had been newly dug.[36]

It was under Emma's direction that false coffins filled with sand were buried on the hillside near the temple. She knew that enemies of the Prophet had set a price on his body, and she was afraid that someone would violate his grave for the ransom money. Emma was right. Just twelve days after the "mock" funeral, thieves broke into the burial place and "found only sand in the coffins. The news spread rapidly. This prompted Emma" to consider "an even more secret reburial."[37]

Some time later, Emma had the bodies of Joseph and Hyrum removed from the first burial place, which was the basement of the Nauvoo House, to another "secret" burial place that she thought would be much safer. The exact place of this reburial was known only to Emma and the men who helped Emma with the reburial. Even Emma's children did not know the exact place where their father was buried, so they also called it the "Unknown Grave." Many years later, when Emma's son, David Hyrum, had grown to manhood, he wrote the following poem, which has been set to music:

THE UNKNOWN GRAVE

There's an unknown grave in a green, lowly spot,
The form that it covers will ne'er be forgot,
Where haven trees spread and the wild locusts wave
Their fragrant white blooms o'er the unknown grave,—
  O'er the unknown grave.

And nearby its side does the wild rabbit tread,
While over its bosom the wild thistles spread,
As if, in their kindness, to guard and to save
From man's footstep, intruding, the unknown grave,—
  Guarding the unknown grave.

The heavens may weep and the thunders moan low,
Or the bright sun shine, and the soft breezes blow;
Unheeding the heart, once responsive and brave,
Of the one who sleeps there in the unknown grave,—
  Low in an unknown grave.

The prophet whose life was destroyed by his foes
Sleeps now where no hand may disturb his repose
'Til the trumpets of God drown the notes of the wave
And we see him arise from his unknown grave,—
  God bless that unknown grave.

The love all-embracing that never can end,
In death, as in life, knew him well as a friend;
The power of Jesus, the mighty to save,
Will despoil of its treasure the unknown grave,—
No more an unknown grave.[38]

At the time Emma had the bodies of Joseph and Hyrum removed from the basement of the Nauvoo House to the "Unknown Grave" she had one of the men who was helping with the reburial cut a lock of hair from Joseph's head. As Emma requested, he gave it to her. Emma put it in the locket of a brooch pin, and she wore it in remembrance of her beloved husband, the Prophet Joseph Smith.[39]

In the romantic, sentimental nineteenth century in which Emma and Joseph lived, it was quite common for young people in love to exchange locks of their hair to show their devotion to each other. This is described in Elizabeth Barrett Browning's *Sonnets from the Portuguese*, Sonnets XVIII and XIX.[40] Elizabeth Barrett explains how she and her sweetheart, Robert Browning, exchanged locks of hair. After Elizabeth received the gift of a lock of Robert Browning's hair, she romantically told him that she would "lay it on her heart" so that it would not lack any natural heat until her heart grew cold in death. Perhaps this is what Emma thought when she wore the brooch pin which contained the lock of hair from the head of her beloved husband.

IX

"Sweet My Child, I Live For Thee"

No coward soul is mine,
No trembler in the world's
storm-troubled sphere:
I see Heaven's glories shine,
And Faith shines equal,
arming me from Fear.

—*Emily Bronte*

The hostilities towards the Latter-day Saints in Nauvoo didn't end after the martyrdom of the Prophet Joseph Smith. Just as in Missouri, the mandate of the mob was for the Mormons to leave the state of Illinois or be "exterminated!" The Saints, under the new leadership of Brigham Young, chose to leave

Illinois. Brigham Young's energy was exerted in getting the Saints across the Mississippi River and into the Iowa territory. Emma decided to stay in Nauvoo with her children rather than go with the exiled Saints to the wilderness of the West under the leadership of Brigham Young.

Considering the hostility towards the Latter-day Saints in and around Nauvoo, Emma's decision to remain in Nauvoo and take care of her children alone showed great fortitude and courage.

Why did Emma decide to stay in Nauvoo and face the hostilities there instead of going with her friends across the Mississippi River? Her friends in the Church invited and urged her to go with them, but she refused. One reason was that she detested the practice of plural marriage and she knew that this "ancient principle" was being practiced in secret by the leaders of the Church. Another reason was that although her husband was dead, she wanted to live near his grave which, though unknown to others, was known to her. Then when her own death would come, she could be buried near her beloved husband, the Prophet Joseph Smith.

Emma sacrificed the love of her family when she married Joseph. Emma loved her mother and father and her brothers and sisters dearly, but she was willing to sacrifice the love of her family because of a greater love and devotion for Joseph. It was not that she loved her family less than she did before she met and married Joseph, it was only that she had a greater love for Joseph, and she was not willing to give up her love for him for the continued love of her family. Emma's family was "so disappointed that Emma had married Joseph Smith that they practically crossed her name off the family roster. Even after the martyrdom of Joseph Smith they were reluctant to fellowship his widow in the lonely Mansion House in the deserted city" of Nauvoo.[1]

After the martyrdom of the Prophet Joseph Smith and before the birth of David Hyrum, Emma made an attempt to be reconciled with her sister Elizabeth, who lived in Dixon, Illinois. Emma went to visit her sister, but she "was not made welcome in her sister's home. After a short and unhappy visit she returned to Nauvoo. As she placed her children [Julia, Joseph III, Frederick and Alexander] in the carriage she said to them, 'We have no place [to go] but home, and no friend but God!'"[2]

In October, 1832, twelve years before this unhappy visit with her sister Elizabeth, Emma had had a similar experience, but it was not as hurtful, because at that time Emma had "one true and living friend on earth"–her husband. Following is an excerpt from a letter Joseph wrote to Emma shortly before the birth of Joseph III:

> I feel as if I wanted to say something to you to comfort you in your peculiar trial and present afflic-tion. I hope God will give you strength that you may not faint. I pray God to soften the hearts of those

around you to be kind to you and take the burden off your shoulders as much as possible and not afflict you. I feel for you for I know your state and that others do not, but you must comfort your-self knowing that God is your friend in Heaven and that you have one true and living friend on earth, your husband.[3]

Emma must have been very sad when she said to her children as she left her sister's home, "We have no place [to go] but home, and no friend but God."[4] But Emma still had much to live for. Although her "true and living friend on earth," her husband, had been martyred, she still had the blessing of her children and the comfort of her God. She also had the blessing of a home to go to where she could take care of her children, and together they could love and worship God.

On November 17, 1844, almost five months after the death of her husband, Emma gave birth to another baby boy, whom she named David Hyrum, as the Prophet Joseph Smith had requested before his martyrdom. After little David Hyrum was born, Emma had five young children to support and take care of: Julia, Joseph III, Frederick, Alexander, and little David Hyrum. Emma had given birth to five other children: one did not survive his birth, three lived only a short time, and darling little Don Carlos died when he was just fourteen months old.

When opposition against the Mormons in Nauvoo became too great, Emma left Nauvoo with her children and went up the river to live in Fulton, Illinois, until things could become more peaceful in Nauvoo. While she was gone she rented the Mansion House to Mr. Van Tuyl, one of the "new citizens" in Nauvoo. Emma lived in Fulton for five months—from September to February—when she found out that Mr. Van Tuyl was planning to go to Texas and take the furnishings of the Mansion House with him. Emma, knowing that this would require her personal attention, bundled up her children and traveled overland to Nauvoo. When she arrived at the Mansion House she surprised Mr. Van Tuyl. Although she lost the rent money which Mr. Van Tuyl had not paid her, she was able to recover most of the furnishings of the Mansion House.

Emma did not return to Fulton, because the "exiled" Latter-day Saints, under the leadership of Brigham Young, had left Nauvoo, and there was a more peaceful atmosphere there. Emma felt that she could manage her Mansion House as a hotel in peace and use the income from it to support her children.

In the summer of 1847, three years after the death of her husband, Emma became acquainted with another of the "new citizens" of Nauvoo, Lewis Bidamon. Mr. Bidamon began calling at the Mansion House with the amorous intention of courting the widow of the Prophet Joseph Smith. He was a tall handsome man of German descent, with dark hair and eyes, a widower from Canton, Illinois, where he had buried his wife and his only son, before coming to Nauvoo. He was a friendly person with a charming personality. However, he was not very spiritually inclined, and he had a bad drinking habit. When Lewis Bidamon was courting his mother, young Joseph III was fourteen years old. Following is a little incident of the courtship which Joseph III found rather amusing:

[Mr. Bidamon] came courting one day at the Mansion House, dressed in his newest raiment like a prosperous keeper of vineyards. He left his team in the barnyard, and walked past the old well near the back of the house. He kept looking toward the windows, hoping to see the young widow before he knocked at the door, to allow her a preview of himself as the dashing, dressy, gallant suitor as he ambled toward the house. When he finally saw her seated by the window sewing, he waved an affectionate greeting. Then he removed his tall hat, making a polite sweeping bow as he uncovered his head. Erect again and his hat in place, he continued to watch the lady of his choice as he walked directly under the clothes line which swept off his tall hat as well as his toupee which had concealed a large bald spot.

This incident was a source of great embarrassment to [Mr. Bidamon] . . . but one of great amusement to Joseph and Alexander who were playing in the yard and watching as Mr. Bidamon came to serenade his lady.[5]

This courtship resulted in a proposal for marriage about six months later. Lewis Bidamon and Emma were married about three and one-half years after the death of the Prophet Joseph Smith.

Although Lewis Bidamon was not a religious man, he was helpful and kind to Emma and her children. He owned a small store in Nauvoo, in which two of Emma's sons found employment.

Lewis Bidamon was a handyman around the house. He was skilled in the use of tools, having once been a saddle maker. He was able to build nice pieces of furniture for the house and make the needed household repairs. He was also skilled in farming and helping Emma and her children with the large vegetable garden which they needed to provide food for her growing family. All in all, Lewis Bidamon, in spite of his intemperate habits and his lack of religion, was a good man to have around the house.

Emma's love for the Prophet Joseph Smith did not die with his martyrdom. She hung on to his memory through certain relics. For example, when Wilford Woodruff visited Emma, "she gave him a piece of oak for a staff. The oak had been taken from Joseph's coffin."[6] She also hung on to the memory of her dead husband with the lock of his hair she wore in the locket of a brooch pin.

Another precious possession Emma kept for her martyred husband was the manuscript he had made of the "Inspired Version" of the Bible. On February 15, 1839, when Emma crossed the frozen Mississippi River into Quincy, Illinois, to be an exile with other Latter-day Saints there, she carried her two younger children in her arms; her two older children clung to her skirts, and under the folds of her skirts, in two cotton bags attached to her waist, she carried this precious manuscript. At this time her Prophet husband was a prisoner in the Liberty Jail in Missouri.

Emma kept this precious manuscript of the Inspired Version of the Bible with her in the Mansion House. She had seen the beautiful Nauvoo Temple burn because of a fire started by a mobbish arsonist. Emma had a feeling that the Mansion House would never be burned by fire, because the Mansion House contained this sacred manuscript on which the Prophet Joseph Smith had worked so diligently before his death.

In 1866, when Emma's son, Joseph III, was President of the Reorganized Church of Jesus Christ of Latter Day Saints, she gave this manuscript to that church for publication. It was published in 1867 by the RLDS Church as the "Inspired Version" of the Holy Scriptures. This "translation" has been very useful and valuable to both the RLDS Church and the LDS Church in clearing up points of doctrine. It has also helped in the restoration of many "plain and precious" things that have been left out of the Holy Scriptures.

Emma's Deathbed Vision

"Emma, come with me." "It is time for you to come with me."
"As she turned her face and gazed upward, her last words
were: 'Yes, yes! I am coming!'—as if she saw or heard someone
beckoning or calling her."[1]

X

"Emma, Come With Me"

"Emma, be patient, and you shall have all of your children."

—*Joseph Smith*

*E*mma's children grew to maturity, married and left home, but Emma was always ready to help them in times of need. Her son Joseph III said that his mother was always helpful but never interfering. She was there to help him when his young wife, Emmeline, died, leaving him with three small children.

Emma helped in caring for Emmeline during her illness and death, and also in caring for her children until Joseph III married again.

Emma also took care of her mother-in-law (the Prophet's mother, Lucy Mack Smith) when she was old and disabled. Emma's second husband, Lewis Bidamon, was also very kind and considerate of the Prophet Joseph Smith's mother, who lived with Emma and him until her death. With his skill in the use of tools, Lewis Bidamon devised a wheelchair for Emma's mother-in-law to make her last days more comfortable.[2] Like an angel of mercy, Emma took care of Lucy during the last years of her life and during her last illness. Then she gently "laid her to rest." In his book about Joseph Smith's family, E. Cecil McGavin says:

> "An eternal benediction of gratitude is due Emma for her kindness to this grand old lady who lived eleven years after the martyrdom of her two sons."[3]

When the Prophet Joseph Smith's father, Joseph Smith, Sr., was patriarch of the Church, he gave Emma her patriarchal blessing, which said to her, "Thou shalt see many days, yea, the Lord will spare thee till thou art satisfied." On April 30, 1879, Emma had seen many days, and she was satisfied. She was ready to go to her "eternal reward."[4] Her living children gathered around her bedside, grieving because they knew she was dying. Following is what happened at the time of her death, as told by her son, Alexander:

Just before she passed away she called, "Joseph, Joseph." I thought she meant my brother. He was in the room, and I spoke to him and said, "Joseph, Mother wants you." I was at the head of the bed. My mother raised right up, lifted her left hand as high as she could raise it, and called, "Joseph." I put my left arm around her shoulders, took her hand in mine, saying, "Mother, what is it?" I laid her hand on her bosom, and she was dead; she had passed away.

When I asked of her calling "Joseph" to Sister Revel, who was with us, Sister Revel said, "A short time before she died she had a vision which she related to me. She said that your father came to her and said to her, 'Emma, come with me, it is time for you to come with me.' And as she related it she said, 'I put on my bonnet and my shawl and went with him; I did not think that it was anything unusual. I went with him into a mansion, a beautiful mansion, and he showed me through the different apartments of that beautiful mansion. And one room was the nursery. In that nursery was a babe in the cradle.' She said, 'I knew my babe, my Don Carlos that was taken from me.' She sprang forward, caught the child up in her arms and wept with joy over the child. When she recovered sufficiently she turned to Joseph, and said, 'Where are the rest of my children?' He said to her, 'Emma, be patient, and you shall have all of your children.'"[5]

Epilogue

The respect, esteem, and love with which Emma was regarded by all is but a just tribute to her sterling virtues.

—*The Nauvoo Newspaper*

A devoted wife in the sentimental nineteenth century usually had one last wish or request, which was to be buried near her beloved husband. A good example of this is the Prophet Joseph Smith's mother, Lucy Mack Smith. When Brigham Young with his loyal Latter-day Saints left Nauvoo to "go away to the west," he asked Joseph Smith's mother to go with them. She seemed to be willing to go, but she had one last request. The following is in her own words:

> "Here in this city, lay my dead: my husband and children; . . . If I go, I want my bones brought back in case I die away, and deposited with my husband and children."[1]

The Prophet Joseph Smith's mother decided not to go with Brigham Young and the main body of the Latter-day Saints. She decided to stay in Nauvoo. Emma took care of her in her feeble last years and fulfilled her request of being buried near her husband and children.

In a like manner, Emma wanted to be buried near her beloved husband when her time on earth ended. Before her death, Emma told her sons where she wanted to be buried. Obviously, this would be near the "Unknown Grave" of her beloved husband, their father. Emma's last request was fulfilled by her sons after her funeral.

The news of Emma's death brought sorrow to the people of Nauvoo, especially to Emma's neighbors who knew her and loved her. To the children she was known as the "cookie lady," because of the many times she had baked cookies and had given them to the children in her neighborhood.

Following is an excerpt from the sermon given at Emma's funeral:

> In her youth she gave her heart and hand to a poor young man. By this act she invited the displea-

sure of her family. For a brief season they received
her back, then turned from her again, and she
accompanied her husband to the western wilds. They
resided for a season in Ohio, then farther west we
see her standing side by side with her companion
while surrounded by a hostile foe. Again we behold
her, as in tears and bitter anguish she sees her
husband torn from her by a ruthless mob and
dragged away to prison and prospective death. She is
left in poverty and distress, and being no longer able
to remain near her husband because of the cruel
edict of an inhuman executive, she turns her face
eastward and with her little children faces the pitiless
winter storm. On foot she crosses the ice of the
Father of Waters, her two youngest children in her
arms, the other two clinging to her dress. Then in
anguish and suspense she awaits tidings from her
husband, whom she has left in a dungeon surrounded by cruel foes. If in all this she ever murmured or
faltered in her devotion, we know it not.

At length he joins her and a brief season of
repose is granted them, during which she sees her
husband rise to eminence and distinction, and she,
as she was commanded, delights in the glory that
came to him. But, alas! This is only the calm before
the storm. Again, the heavy, cruel hand of persecution is upon them, and upon a calm summer day
they bear to her home the mutilated body of her
murdered husband. Thousands pass the bier, and
look for the last time on the face of the honored
dead. Then she gathers her children around that

silent form, and looks upon those calm lips which had in time of trouble pronounced those words so full of pathos and love, "My beloved Emma, choice of my heart. . . . Again she is here, even in the seventh trouble—undaunted, firm, and unwavering—unchangeable, affectionate Emma." And from her full heart cries, "My husband, Oh! my husband, have they taken you from me, at last! . . ."

Was it not her loving hand, her consoling and comforting words, her unswerving integrity, fidelity, and devotions, her wise counsel, that assisted to make this latter-day work a success? If God raised up a Joseph as a prophet and a restorer of the Gospel truth, then did he raise up an Emma as a helpmeet for him.[2]

The Nauvoo Newspaper carried a long article about Emma's death. Excerpts from this article follow:

After the services were over, the large company filed through the room past the coffin, viewing the face of the deceased as they passed. It was a touching sight to see those citizens so long acquainted with the silent sleeper, while she was living, pausing beside her to take a last look at her peaceful face, so calm amid the grief of the assembly. Now and then one to whom she had been dearer than to others would press the extended hand, or gently stooping lay a hand upon the cold face or forehead, some even kissing the pale cheek in an impulse of love and regret.

But scenes of grief must pass—the family at last took leave of her whom they had so long known and loved. The coffin lid was put in place. The six bearers raised their burden reverently, and with the mourning train, passed to the place of interment upon the premises of her eldest son, near by, where with solemn hymn and fervent prayer the remains were left to their long repose.

The assembly was large: almost everyone knew Mrs. Bidamon, some intimately and for many years; some but for a few months, but it is safe to say that the respect, esteem, and love with which she was regarded by all is but a just tribute to the sterling virtues of the woman, wife, and mother, whom the community so soberly, so sadly, and so tenderly laid away to rest, on that beautiful May day, by the side of the Father of Waters, the mighty Mississippi.[3]

For almost fifty years, Emma "slumbered in death" beside a lilac bush near the grave of her beloved husband. Then in 1928 her grandson, Frederick M. Smith, had the graves of Emma, Joseph and Hyrum opened, and reburied near the old Homestead. The Prophet Joseph Smith was reburied, with Emma on his right side and Hyrum on his left side. Then a slab of concrete was placed over the graves, with an inscription marking each grave.

On December 2, 1867, Emma wrote a letter to her son, Joseph III, saying,

"I have always felt sad about the neglected condition of that place [the Smith Family Cemetery]. . . . I have got twenty-five dollars that no one else has any right to but myself. . . . I feel anxious to apply that money on the graveyard. After I have done that I think we can ask our Smith relations to help mark Father's and Mother's graves, if no more."[4]

This plea from Emma encouraged the descendants of Joseph Smith, Sr., and Lucy Mack Smith to renovate and landscape the old neglected Smith Family Cemetery in Nauvoo.

In 1990 "Descendants of the Smith family formed the Joseph and Hyrum Smith Family Foundation with the goal of improving the historic cemetery."[5] In 1991, the slab of concrete which had marked the graves of Emma, Joseph, and Hyrum from 1928 to 1991 was replaced by a beautiful large granite headstone. "Trees, grass and flowers were planted, brick walkways, teak wood benches and a lighting system were installed and a new fence was built around the Homestead and graveyard area."[6]

The cemetery was dedicated on August 4, 1991. About two hundred descendants of Joseph and Hyrum and more than eight hundred other people attended the dedication. "Pres. Wallace B. Smith, president of the Reorganized Church of Jesus Christ of Latter Day Saints dedicated the cemetery, which is located on RLDS property. He is a great-grandson of Joseph [and Emma] Smith."[7]

Elder M. Russell Ballard, a great-great-grandson of Hyrum Smith and a member of the Quorum of the Twelve Apostles of The Church of Jesus Christ of Latter-day Saints, said: "I am sure there will be personal joy and satisfaction for each one of us in knowing that we helped provide a pleasing resting place from which these great ancestors of ours can rise on the morning of the resurrection."[8]

The burial place of Joseph, Emma, and Hyrum Smith in Nauvoo, Illinois. In the background is the Homestead.

Notes

CHAPTER I–THE VISIONS

1. Alfred Lord Tennyson, "Idylls of the King," in *The Best of Tennyson*, ed. Walter Graham (New York: The Ronald Press Company, 1940), 606.

2. John A. Widstoe, *Joseph Smith* (Salt Lake City: Deseret News Press, 1951), 35.

3. Margaret Wilson Gibson, *Emma Smith* (Independence, Missouri: Harold House, 1976), 31.

4. Ivan J. Barrett, *Joseph Smith and the Restoration* (Provo, Utah: Brigham Young University Press, 1973), 71.

5. Buddy Youngreen, *Reflections of Emma* (Orem, Utah: Keepsake Paper Backs, 1982), 5.

6. The Pearl of Great Price, rev. ed. (Salt Lake City, Utah: The Church of Jesus Christ of Latter-day Saints, 1986), Joseph Smith History, 1:57.

CHAPTER II—THE GOLDEN PLATES

1. The Pearl of Great Price, JSH, 1:53, 54.

2. Lucy Mack Smith, *History of Joseph Smith by His Mother, Lucy Mack Smith*, ed. Preston Nibley (Salt Lake City: Bookcraft, 1956), 110.

3. Barrett, *Joseph Smith and the Restoration*, 77.

4. E. Cecil McGavin, *The Family of Joseph Smith* (Salt Lake City: Bookcraft, 1963), 118.

5. Ibid., 119-20.

6. Roy A. Cheville, *Joseph and Emma Smith, Companions* (Independence, Missouri: Herald Publishing House, 1977), 22.

7. Lucy Mack Smith, *History of Joseph Smith*, 133-35.

8. Cheville, *Joseph and Emma*, 32.

9. Lucy Mack Smith, *History of Joseph Smith*, 152.

CHAPTER III—THE "ELECT LADY"

1. Joseph Smith, *History of The Church of Jesus Christ of Latter-day Saints* (Salt Lake City: Deseret Book Company, 1956), 1:84.

2. Ibid., 1:86.

3. Ibid., 1:87-88.

4. Ibid., 1:106.

5. Ibid., 1:108.

6. Elizabeth Barrett Browning, *Sonnets from the Portuguese* (New York: Thomas Y. Crowell Company, 1943), 73.

7. Truman G. Madsen, *Joseph Smith the Prophet* (Salt Lake City, Utah: Bookcraft, 1989), 30.

8. Ivan J. Barrett, *Heroines of the Church* (Provo, Utah: Brigham Young University Publications, 1966), 35-36.

9. McGavin, *The Family of Joseph Smith*, 124.

10. Lucy Mack Smith, *History of Joseph Smith*, 190-91.

CHAPTER IV—KIRTLAND

1. Lucy Mack Smith, *History of Joseph Smith*, 218-21.

2. Youngreen, *Reflections of Emma*, 14.

3. McGavin, *The Family of Joseph Smith*, 130-31.

4. Vesta Crawford, Papers, box 2, folder 1, Brigham Young University Library, Provo, Utah.

5. Brent L. Top, "I Was With My Family," *Ensign*, August 1991, 26.

6. Gracia N. Jones, *Emma's Glory and Sacrifice* (Hurricane, Utah: Homestead Publishers and Distributors, 1987), 45.

7. Joseph Smith, *History of the Church*, 2:414.

8. Ibid., 2:428.

9. Ibid., 2:428.

CHAPTER V—FAR WEST

1. Ibid. 3:1.

2. Ibid. 3:2.

3. Ibid. 3:8.

4. Ibid. 3:8-9.

5. Ibid. 3:175.

6. Ibid. 3:182

7. Ibid. 3:193-94.

8. Ibid. 3:201.

9. Youngreen, *BYU Studies* 14 (Winter, 1974): 210.

10. Dean C. Jessee, ed., *The Personal Writings of Joseph Smith* (Salt Lake City: Deseret Book, 1984), 362-63.

11. Youngreen, *Reflections of Emma*, 22-23.

12. McGavin, *The Family of Joseph Smith*, 158-59.

13. Ibid., 158-60.

14. Ibid., 160-61.

15. Ibid., 162.

16. Mary Audentia Smith Anderson, ed., *Joseph III and the Restoration* (Independence, Missouri: Herald Publishing House, 1952) 12.

CHAPTER VI–NAUVOO

1. Cheville, *Joseph and Emma*, 79.

2. Emma Smith to Joseph Smith, March 9, 1839 (Provo, Utah: Brigham Young University, microfilm, MSS Film #2, Joseph Smith Collection, Reel #2, Letters, 1839).

3. Joseph Smith, *History of the Church*, 3:327.

4. David E. Miller and Della S. Miller, *Nauvoo: The City of Joseph* (Santa Barbara and Salt Lake City: Peregrine Smith, Inc., 1974), 26.

5. Joseph Smith, *History of the Church*, 4:19.

6. Ibid., 4:80.

7. Jones, *Emma's Glory*, 107.

8. Joseph Smith, *History of the Church*, 4:365.

9. Ibid., 4:366.

10. Ibid., 4:369-70.

11. Ibid., 4:370.

12. Ibid., 4:371.

13. Ibid., 4:371.

14. Ibid., 4:371.

15. Youngreen, *Reflections of Emma*, 25.

16. Preston Nibley, *Joseph Smith, the Prophet* (Salt Lake City: Deseret News Press, 1946), 378.

17. Joseph Smith, *History of the Church*, 4:552-53.

18. Ibid., 4:605.

19. Ibid., 4:607.

20. Ibid., 5:14.

21. Ibid., 5:86.

22. Ibid., 5:107.

23. Ibid., 5:92.

24. Ibid., 5:103.

25. Ibid., 5:114.

26. Ibid., 5:117-18.

27. Ibid., 5:160.

28. Ibid., 5:137.

29. Ibid., 5:115.

30. Ibid., 5:118.

31. Ibid., 5:166-68.

32. Ibid., 5:182-83.

33. Ibid., 5:204-5.

34. Ibid., 5:231.

35. Ibid., 5:247-8.

36. Ibid., 6:134.

37. Joseph III 74-76.

38. Josiah Quincy was the President of Harvard University in Boston.

39. Anderson, *Joseph III*, 48.

CHAPTER VII–"MARRIAGE IS ORDAINED OF GOD"

1. Francis M. Gibbons, *Joseph Smith, Martyr, Prophet of God* (Salt Lake City: Deseret Book Company, 1977), 307.

2. Youngreen, *Reflections of Emma*, 31.

3. Barrett, *Joseph Smith and the Restoration*, 520-21.

4. Youngreen, *Reflections of Emma*, 32.

5. Barrett, *Joseph Smith and the Restoration*, 526.

6. Russell Rich, *Ensign to the Nations* (Provo, Utah: Brigham Young University Press, 1978), 205.

7. Ibid., 366.

8. Ibid., 378.

9. Doctrine and Covenants of The Church of Jesus Christ of Latter-day Saints, rev. ed. (Salt Lake City: The Church of Jesus Christ of Latter-day Saints, 1986), Official Declaration–1 and "Excerpts from three addresses by President Wilford regarding the Manifesto," 291-93.

CHAPTER VIII—"HOME THEY BROUGHT HER WARRIOR DEAD"

1. Barrett, *Joseph Smith and the Restoration*, 521.

2. Doctrine and Covenants, 132:1.

3. The Book of Mormon: Another Testament of Jesus Christ, trans. Joseph Smith, Jr., rev. ed. (Salt Lake City: The Church of Jesus Christ of Latter-day Saints, 1986), Jacob 2:24.

4. George W. Given, *In Old Nauvoo* (Salt Lake City: Deseret Book, 1990), 211. Emphases added.

5. Youngreen, *Reflections of Emma*, 31.

6. Joseph Smith, *History of the Church*, 6:430.

7. Ibid., 6:432.

8. Governor Carlin was replaced by the newly-elected Governor Ford.

9. Joseph Smith, *History of the Church*, 6:545-46.

10. Ibid., 6:546.

11. Ibid., 6:549-50.

12. Ibid., 6:551-52

13. Ibid., 6:554.

14. Doctrine and Covenants, 135:4.

15. Joseph Smith, *History of the Church*, 6:556.

16. Ibid., 6:558.

17. Jones, *Emma's Glory*, 153.

18. Joseph Smith, *History of the Church*, 6:565. A letter Joseph wrote to Emma dated June 25, 1844, states: "Myself

and Hyrum have been again arrested for treason because we called out the Nauvoo Legion."

19. Joseph Smith, *History of the Church*, 6:580.

20. Ibid., 6:605.

21. Ibid., 6:600.

22. Ibid., 6:600.

23. Ibid., 6:617.

24. Ibid., 6:617.

25. Ibid., 6:618.

26. Ibid., 6:618.

27. Ibid., 6:619.

28. Ibid., 6:621.

29. Ibid., 6:626.

30. Alfred Lord Tennyson, "Lyrics from the Princess," in *The Best of Tennyson*, ed. Walter Graham (New York: The Ronald Press Company, 1940), 150.

31. Joseph Smith, *History of the Church*, 6:627.

32. Youngreen, *Reflections of Emma*, 36.

33. Lucy Mack Smith, *History of Joseph Smith*, 325.

34. Joseph Smith, *History of the Church*, 6:627.

35. Ibid., 6:627-28.

36. Ibid., 6:628.

37. Cheville, *Joseph and Emma*, 115.

38. McGavin, *The Family of Joseph Smith*, 265-66.

39. Anderson, *Joseph III*, 85.

40. Browning, *Sonnets*, 40-41.

CHAPTER IX—"SWEET MY CHILD, I LIVE FOR THEE"

1. McGavin, *The Family of Joseph Smith*, 291.
2. Ibid., 200.
3. Ibid., 131.
4. Ibid., 200.
5. Ibid., 174.
6. Matthias F. Cowley, *Wilford Woodruff* (Salt Lake City: Bookcraft, 1965), 227.

CHAPTER X—"EMMA, COME WITH ME"

1. Anderson, *Joseph III*, 283.
2. McGavin, *The Family of Joseph Smith*, 176.
3. Ibid., 241-42.
4. Emma was sealed to Joseph "for time and all eternity" on May 28, 1843. When Emma was in her 75th year of life, she had seen "many days." Apparently she was satisfied and it was time for her to see Joseph again.
5. Alexander Hale Smith, "Second Coming of Christ," *Zion's Ensign* 31 (December 1903): 7. This is a sermon given at Bottineau, N.D., July 1, 1903, reported by L. A. Gould. A microfilm copy of the sermon is in the Brigham Young University Library.

EPILOGUE

1. Joseph Smith, *History of the Church*, 7:471.

2. McGavin, *The Family of Joseph Smith*, 184-86.

3. Ibid., 188-89.

4. Sheridan R. Sheffield, "Cemetery dedication a fulfill-ment of dreams," *Deseret News*, 10 Aug. 1991, Church News Section.

5. "Smith Descendants Improve Nauvoo Burial Ground," *Ensign*, August 1991: 77.

6. Sheffield, "Cemetery dedication."

7. Ibid.

8. "Smith Descendants:" 78.

Bibliography

Anderson, Mary Audentia Smith, ed. *Joseph III and the Restoration*. Independence, Missouri: Herald Publishing House, 1952.

Andrus, Hyrum L. *Joseph Smith, The Man and the Seer*. Salt Lake, Utah: Deseret Book Company, 1960.

Barrett, Ivan J. *Joseph Smith and the Restoration*. Provo, Utah: Brigham Young University Press, 1973.

_____. *Heroines of the Church*. Provo, Utah: Brigham Young University Publications, 1966.

Beecher, Maureen Ursenbach. *Eliza and Her Sisters*. Salt Lake City, Utah: Aspen Books, 1991.

_____. and James L. Kimball, Jr. "The First Relief Society." Salt Lake City, Utah: *Ensign* Magazine, March 1979, 25-29.

Berrett, William E. *The Restored Church*. Salt Lake City, Utah: Deseret Book Company, 1965.

Book of Mormon, Salt Lake City, Utah: The Church of Jesus Christ of Latter-day Saints, 1979.

Brodie, Fawn M. *No Man Knows My History*. New York: Alfred A. Knopf, 1946.

Browning, Elizabeth Barrett. *Sonnets from the Portuguese*. New York: Thomas Y. Crowell Company, 1936.

Cheville, Roy A. *Joseph and Emma Smith, Companions*. Independence, Missouri: Herald Publishing House, 1977.

Cowley, Matthias F., ed. *Wilford Woodruff, History of His Life and Labors*. Salt Lake City, Utah: Bookcraft, 1964.

Crawford, Vesta. *Vesta Crawford Papers*. Brigham Young University Library.

Bibliography

Doctrine and Covenants. Salt Lake City, Utah: The Church of Jesus Christ of Latter-day Saints, 1981.

Evans, John Henry. *Joseph Smith, American Prophet*. New York: Macmillan Co., 1933.

Faulring, Scott H., ed. *Joseph Smith, Diaries and Journals*. Salt Lake City, Utah: Signature Books in association with Smith Research Associates, 1989.

Fischer, Norma J. *Portrait of a Prophet*. Salt Lake City, Utah: Bookcraft, 1960.

Gibbons, Francis M. *Joseph Smith: Martyr, Prophet of God*. Salt Lake City, Utah: Deseret Book Company, 1977.

Gibson, Margaret Wilson. *EMMA SMITH The Elect Lady*. Independence, Missouri: Herald House, 1976.

Givens, George W. *In Old Nauvoo*. Salt Lake City, Utah: Deseret Book Company, 1990.

Hill, Donna. *Joseph Smith: The First Mormon*. Garden City, New York: Doubleday & Co., 1977.

Hymns of The Church of Jesus Christ of Latter-day Saints. Salt Lake City, Utah: Deseret Book Company, 1985.

Jessee, Dean C., ed. *The Personal Writings of Joseph Smith*. Salt Lake City, Utah: Deseret Book, 1984.

Jones, Gracia N. *Emma's Glory and Sacrifice*. Hurricane, Utah: Homestead Publishers and Distributors, 1987.

Madsen, Truman G. *Joseph Smith the Prophet*. Salt Lake City, Utah: Bookcraft, 1989.

McCloud, Susan Evans, *Joseph Smith: A Photo Biography*. Salt Lake City, Utah: Aspen Books, 1992.

McGavin, E. Cecil. *The Family of Joseph Smith*. Salt Lake City, Utah: Bookcraft, 1963.

_____. *Nauvoo, The Beautiful*. Salt Lake City, Utah: Bookcraft, 1972.

Miller, David E. and Della S. Miller, *Nauvoo: The City of Joseph*. Santa Barbara and Salt Lake City: Peregrine Smith, Inc., 1974.

Newell, Linda King and Valeen Tippetts Avery, *Mormon Enigma: Emma Hale Smith*. Garden City, New York: Doubleday & Company, Inc., 1984.

Bibliography

Nibley, Hugh. *No, Ma'am, That's Not History*. Salt Lake City, Utah: Bookcraft, 1946.

Nibley, Preston. *Joseph Smith, The Prophet*. Salt Lake City, Utah: Deseret News Press, 1946.

Oaks, Dallin. "The Suppression of the *Nauvoo Expositor*." Utah Law Review (Winter 1965).

Pearl of Great Price. Salt Lake City, Utah. The Church of Jesus Christ of Latter-day Saints, 1981.

Phillips, Emma M. *Women of the Restoration*. Independence, Missouri: Herald Publishing House, 1960.

Porter, Larry C. "A Study of the Origins of The Church of Jesus Christ of Latter-day Saints in the States of New York and Pennsylvania 1816-1831." Ph.D. Dissertation, Brigham Young University, 1971.

Pratt, Parley P. *Autobiography of Parley P. Pratt*. Salt Lake City, Utah: Deseret Book Company, 1966.

Rich, Russell. *Ensign to the Nations*. Provo, Utah: Brigham Young University Press, 1978.

Sheffield, Sheridan R. "Cemetery dedication a fulfillment of dreams." *Deseret News* 10 Aug. 1991: LDS Church News Section.

"Smith Descendants Improve Nauvoo Burial Ground." *Ensign* (Salt Lake City, Utah) August 1991.

Smith, Emma, compiler. *A Collection of Sacred Hymns for The Church of the Latter Day Saints*. Kirtland, Ohio: F. G. Williams & Co., facsimile copy at Brigham Young University Religion Library.

Smith, Joseph. *History of The Church of Jesus Christ of Latter-day Saints*. 7 Volumes. Edited by B. H. Roberts. Salt Lake City, Utah: Deseret Book Company, 1956.

Smith, Joseph Fielding. *Essentials of Church History*. Salt Lake City, Utah: Deseret Book Co., 1953.

_____. *Teachings of the Prophet Joseph Smith*. Salt Lake City, Utah: Deseret Book Co., 1964.

Smith, Lucy Mack. *History of Joseph Smith by His Mother, Lucy Mack Smith*. Preston Nibley, editor. Salt Lake City, Utah: Bookcraft, 1956.

Bibliography

Tennyson, Alfred Lord. *The Best of Tennyson*. Walter Graham, editor. New York: The Ronald Press Company, 1940.

Terry, Keith & Ann. *The Dramatic Biography of Emma Smith*. Bountiful, Utah: Publishers Book Sales, Inc., 1980.

Van Wagoner, Richard S. *Mormon Polygamy*. Salt Lake City, Utah: Signature Books, 1986.

Widstoe, John A. *Joseph Smith, Seeker After Truth, Prophet of God*. Salt Lake City, Utah: Bookcraft, 1957.

Wirkus, Erwin E. *Judge Me Dear Reader*. Salt Lake City, Utah: Randall Book Company, 1978.

Young, Kimball. *Isn't One Wife Enough*. New York: Henry Holt & Company, 1954.

Youngreen, Buddy. *Joseph and Emma*. Brigham Young University Studies, Volume 14, Number 2, Winter 1974, 199-226.

_____. *Reflections of Emma*. Orem, Utah: Keepsake Paperbacks, 1952.

Index

Abraham, 85
Adam-Ondi-Ahman: hymns, 25
Auge (malarial fever), 55
Ballard, M. Russell, 131
Barrett, Ivan J., 27 *Joseph and the Restoration*, 79
Bawden, Dee Jay: *Emma's Deathbed Vision*; 120
Bernhisel, J. M., 89
Bettisworth, Constable, 98
Bidamon, Lewis: courts Emma Smith 115, 116; helps care for Lucy Mack Smith, 122; marries Emma Smith, 117; store owner and handyman, 117
Boggs, Lilburn W., 48, 57, 70, 71; issues Extermination Order 41; attempted assassination of, 64, 65
Brigham Young University, 27
Browning, Elizabeth Barrett, 26; *Sonnets from the Portuguese*, 109
Browning, O. H., 60
Browning, Robert, 27, 109
Butterfield, Judge, 65; calls on Governor Thomas Ford 71; legal opinion 70, 71
Cahoon, Reynolds, 91; informs Joseph regarding troops 91
Canton, Illinois, 115

Carlin, Thomas, 59
Carthage, 88
Carthage Jail: Joseph and Hyrum confined in, 99
Charity Never Faileth: motto of Relief Society, 64
Church of Jesus Christ of Latter-day Saints, The, 82; dedication of Kirtland Temple, 37; first conference of, 22; hostility toward, 26, 41, 111; hymns of 25; organization of, 19
Clayton, William: 66; calls on Governor Ford, 71; presents Emma's letter to Governor Carlin, 69; transcribes revelation on polygamy, 80
Cleveland, John, 51
Cleveland, Sarah M., 51; 63
Colesville, 22
Columbia, Boone County, 53
Come All Ye Saints of Zion: hymns, 25
Come, All Whose Souls Are Lighted: hymns, 25
Come, All Ye Saints Who Dwell on Earth: hymns, 25
Come Let Us Sing an Evening Hymn: hymns, 25

Index

57; dedication speech of
Kirtland Temple, 37; mobs in
Kirtland cause, to flee, 40;
taken prisoner, 42
Roberts, B. H., 91
Robison, George W., 42
Rockwell, Orrin Porter 92, 94; takes
Joseph and Hyrum into
seclusion, 91; assassination
attempt, 65; sets up bar in
Mansion house, 73;
accompanies Joseph Smith to
Washington, D.C., 57
Rushton, Lettice, 72
Rushton, Richard, 72
Sacrament, 37; revelation regarding,
23, 24
Salt Lake City, Utah: conference
announcing polygamy, 81
Scott, Anne, 50
Smith Family Foundation, Joseph
and Hyrum, 130
Smith, Alexander, 46, 113-114; birth
of, 41; crossed Mississippi
River, 50; relates Emma's
deathbed vision, 123
Smith, Alvin, 12, 31
Smith, David Hyrum, 96, 113; birth
of, 114; *The Unknown Grave*,
108
Smith, Don Carlos, 62, 123; birth
and death of, 58
Smith, Emma Hale, 71; administers
to the sick 55; baptism of, 22;
birth of, 2; blessing from
Joseph, 97-98; burial desires,
126; burial of, 126; cares for
Lucy Mack Smith, 122, 126;
children of, 90—Alexander, 41;

Alvin, 11; David Hyrum, 96,
114; death of, 12; Don Carlos,
58; Frederick, 38; grew to
maturity, 121; Joseph and Julia,
32; Joseph III, 34; stillborn
child, 62; Thaddeus and
Louisa, 29-31;—Christmas for,
71-72; confirmation of, 24;
crosses Mississippi River, 49;
death of, 122; deathbed vision,
123; disputation with Joseph
regarding bar, 73-76; *Emma's
Deathbed Vision* by Dee Jay
Bawden, 120; estranged from
family, 112-113; felt form of
plates, 11; funeral sermon,
126-128; funeral services, 128-
129; good housekeeper and
cook, 35; gravesite, 129; grief
at Joseph's death, 105;
guardian of Inspired Version,
50; helps Joseph III fish, 47;
helps missionaries, 28-29; ill
health, 69-70; leaves Nauvoo
for Fulton, Illinois, 114; letters
from, to Joseph, 44, 51, 91;
letters from Joseph, 34, 44-46,
47, 58, 67, 99, 113; letter to
Governor Carlin, 68-69; letter
to Joseph III regarding
gravesites, 129; lives with
Whitmer family, 26; love for
Joseph, 27-28; manages
Mansion House as hotel, 115;
marries Joseph, 5; marries
Lewis Bidamon, 117; meets
Joseph Smith, 1; motherly love,
51; moves to Kirtland, Ohio,
29; moves to Whitmer home,

16; objects to brethren smoking tobacco, 35; opposition to plural marriage, 77-84, 112; patriarchal blessing, 36-37, 122, 142; praised by Governor Carlin, 69; prays for her father, 2; president of Female Relief Society of Nauvoo, 63; provides for family, 47; purchases furniture in St. Louis, Missouri, 73; receives Joseph's body, 103; remains in Nauvoo, 112; remembers husband, 117-118; revelation regarding, 24; rides beside Joseph in parades, 76; scribe to Joseph, 10, 14; sealed to Joseph, 142; selects hymns, 25; settles with Clevelands, 51; supporter of Joseph, 78; treasures children, 104; tribute from Joseph, 65-66; visits Joseph in hiding, 65, 66-67; visits Joseph in Liberty Jail, 48; wears lock of Joseph's hair in brooch, 109; weeps for Joseph, 43

Smith, Emma, the Elect Lady, of the Restoration by Theodore Gorka, 55

Smith, Emmeline, 121

Smith, Frederick, 45, 47, 113, 114; birth of, 38; crossed Mississippi River, 50

Smith, Frederick M.: moves graves of Emma, Joseph and Hyrum, 129

Smith, George A., 38

Smith, Hyrum: body returned to Nauvoo, 101-102; burial, 106-108; calls on Governor Ford, 71; charged with treason, 98; Christmas visitors, 72; confined in Carthage Jail, 99; death of, 100; discusses polygamy with Emma Smith, 80-81; Doctrine and Covenants 135, tribute to, 105; final hours at Carthage, 99-100; goes into hiding, 90; gravesite moved, 129; Joseph and, surrender, 91-94; Joseph asks advice of, 92; letter to Governor Ford, 92-93; original member of Church, 21; taken prisoner, 42; testimony of, 19

Smith, Joseph, 59; . . . lamb to the slaughter, 95; Hyrum and, surrender, 91-94; accused of attempted assassination, 65; affidavit, 71; angelic visitations to 3, 13-14, 17, 23, 38; baptizes new members, 22; bears testimony in Carthage jail, 99; blesses children, 68; blessing for Emma, 97-98; body returned to Nauvoo, 101-102; borrows baby for Emma, 62-63; burial, 106-108; change of venue, 53; charged with treason, 98; Christmas for, 71-72; collects arms from Nauvoo Legion, 95; comes out of seclusion, 70; confined in Carthage Jail, 99; courtship of Emma Hale, 4; D&C 122, 52; death of, 101; dedication of